A DANGEROUS BALANCING ACT
Amsterdam, Holland 1940-1945

A memoir

Lili Hoffman
&
M. Grunberg

ISBN e-book 978-1-947940-62-8
ISBN audiobook 978-1-947940-67-3
ISBN paperback 978-1-947940-66-6
ISBN hardcover 978-1-947940-68-0

"This story is dedicated to everyone
who puts up a fight against
anti-Semitism, Fascism and Racism."

-Lili Hoffman, Amsterdam 2021

Dear Reader 9

Flash Forward 11

Germany 12

Palma de Mallorca, Spain 1932 19

Amsterdam, Holland 1934 23

Cologne, 1935 24

Holland, 1938 29

War, 1940 32

The German Club 34

The Final Solution 36

Registration 37

Nazi Regulations 38

Segregation 40

Deportations 44

1942 45

Exemptions 47

Fake Papers 51

Fritz 58

The Farmer's Wife 62

Hide 68

Frau Griezell 69

Barbara 80

Elsa 83

The Walls have Ears 91

Split pea soup 94

A Dangerous Balancing Act 95

Final Reckoning 101

Collaborators 107

Liberation Anxiety 109

Liberated 114

Picking up the Pieces 116

Haute Couture 117

The Aftermath 119

***

Dear Reader

This is my life's story. I am not a writer and my memory is fading. I have tried to describe my recollections as accurately as I remember. Some I remember in great detail as if they happened yesterday, others I have a hard time prodding to the surface. I was born in Germany, my parents and grandparents were German. At home we spoke German. I thought nothing of it, until suddenly the government decided we were no longer German. Many books have been written about World War II and for the longest time I didn't think my story was important enough to warrant yet another book. However, having been told countless times on numerous occasions that my story is an unusual one, I'm hoping to offer especially to the younger generation, a glimpse of what it was like hiding in plain sight; living in the city of Amsterdam pretending to be a nazi* from Hitler's *Third Reich*, during the nazi occupation of Holland, which lasted for five very long years, from May 1940 to May 1945.

Amsterdam, Holland
May, 2021

*This word does not deserve the respect of a capital letter

***

Flash Forward

Amsterdam, 1942. It was a typical bleak and wet autumn afternoon. A chill ran down my spine as I hurriedly tried to catch the tram. It was close to five o'clock in the afternoon and I had until eight to get home because of the curfew. Being terribly worried about my mother, I wanted to quickly drop by the address where she was hiding before going home. It was tricky though. I couldn't visit there too often. There were neighbors with prying eyes and in those days, prying eyes were a force to be reckoned with. Their eyes and ears spared no one, especially when there was money to be made by hunting down Jews and reporting them to the police. So, not wanting to compromise my mother's situation, visiting her regularly was out of the question.

Reporting Jews to the authorities for money or benefits such as an extra ration card was a lucrative business.

I hurried across the city center square, the famous *Leidseplein,* and headed towards the tram stop. Suddenly I noticed the sound of footsteps on the cobblestones trailing behind me. As I increased my tempo, so did the footsteps. I was sure I wasn't imagining it, but to avoid any type of confrontation, I didn't want to turn around. Then suddenly I felt two taps on my shoulder. This is it. I'm done for. I turned around. The man I stood face to face with belonged to the dreaded *Grüne Polizei* police force.

I was eighteen years old, Jewish and terrified. And, intensely aware that I couldn't show it.

So miss, where are you headed? I lied and told him that I was on my way home. Can I walk with you? Somewhat relieved, I thought he just wants to flirt a bit. He didn't wait for an answer. What if someone sees me with this guy in his green uniform? Turning the corner, across from the much beloved *Vondelpark*, he stopped in front of a row of typical Amsterdam canal homes. The canal itself had been filled in around the late 1890's, and was now a road adorned on both sides by reverent mature chestnut trees. He stopped and pointed at one of the homes, telling me that's where he lives with a few other gentlemen.

Come on in. I'll make you a cup of coffee.
It sounded more like an order than an invitation. I wasn't sure what to do. If I refused, he would ask for my papers.

I'll come in for a moment, but I do need to get home. It's getting late.

I'll get you home. Don't you worry miss.

Think, I told myself, think!

***

Germany

My father was born in 1899 in Berlin. His liberal Jewish family originally came from Bukovina. Its borders kept changing by wars. It's close to the Ukraine where also today there's a war going on.

Culturally, my father's parents, Moses Hoffman and his wife Julia felt Jewish, but they were not religious. Probably because of that, neither were we religious at home.

My maternal grandparents, on the other hand kept a religious lifestyle. Every Friday evening and Saturday morning, my mother's parents Nathan and grandma Lea visited the synagogue. Together they had seven children; two sons died in World War I and son Fritz, and four daughters; Mina, Ella, Lotte and Frieda. Frieda became my mother. Grandpa Nathan died shortly after I was born and Grandma Lea died in 1941, in a retirement home in Cologne. Lucky for her she died a natural death just before the Holocaust. Had she lived, she would have been deported in a cattle car and sent to her death. My mother's sister Lotte and her husband Josef were deported to Krakow and murdered during the Holocaust. Their children Bernard, Ruth and Ingrid managed to make it out of Germany and immigrated 1939, just in time, to the United States.

In 1794, France occupied the city of Cologne on the Rhine River. The region became part of Napoleon's Empire. In 1801, citizens of Cologne were granted French citizenship. The French occupation ended in 1814, when Cologne was occupied by Prussian and Russian troops. From the end of World War I, from 1918 until 1926, Cologne was occupied by the British Army under the terms of the Peace Treaty of Versailles. In contrast with the harsh French, the Brits were more lenient to the local population. The British left in 1926 and in 1933, the Cologne democratic parties lost the elections to the extreme right nazi-party.

My mother Frieda was born in 1899 in the city of Cologne, the same year as my father. She had a tough childhood. She lost two of her brothers in World War I and in World War II, she lost two sisters and brothers-in-law. My parents were married in 1921, in the city of Koblenz, Germany. In 1923 they moved to Cologne, where my brother Hans was born one year ahead of me. Our family and Grandma Lea lived next door to each other. We had separate front doors. On Fridays, we unusually ate dinner at Grandma Lea's next door, because she kept kosher and we didn't. It was easier that way.

My mother was soft spoken and devoted to my father, my brother and me. She kept house, cooked and cared lovingly for the three of us. Sparingly, when my father would take Hans and me to the zoo or we'd go feed the ducks in the park, my mother would get together with her sisters and catch a movie at the local cinema house or watch an opera or play at the theater. She loved music and knew a lot about it. She could name the classical composers and knew the names of the operas and the arias on the radio. She sang along with the librettos without fail.

I was born August 11, 1924 in the city of Cologne, about 150 miles south east of the city of Amsterdam, Holland. In 1930, when I was six years old we still lived in Cologne. I attended the same

Jewish primary school as my nieces and nephews. On Saturdays the school was closed. I attended this school until 1932, the year that Hitler became a household name.

In 1922, Hitler's rise to fame had started gradually after his release from prison. You heard something here, read something there, while all along the German people as a whole increasingly started showing an openly hostile attitude towards Jews. Cologne had become the center of the National Socialists; the behavior of its members was marked by anti-Semitism and extreme violence. Anti-Semitic agitation, propaganda and violent attacks on Jews and Jewish institutions became commonplace. Many German Jews fled. The most well known are probably Albert Einstein and Hollywood directors Fritz Lang, Ernst Lubitsch and Billy Wilder.

Many of my parents' Jewish friends and acquaintances began to apply for passports and visas so they could leave. In reality, they fled. When anti-Semitism became so blatant and shamelessly sanctioned, my father decided to leave Cologne. First we moved to the town of Düsseldorf. I was eight or nine years old at the time. I don't know why we moved to Düsseldorf. It was close to Cologne. It would be the first move of many.

The rule at home was my father's rule. In those days, it was a given that father knew best.

So one day in 1932, when my father quite unexpectedly sent my mother, Hans and me to

Spain, we did what we were told. The day before our departure, he sat us down.

Germany has gotten too dangerous for us, he said. Your mother and I think it is better if we go and live in Spain for a while. It's easier to get papers for Spain than America. I'll wrap things up here and follow you there.

It came totally unexpected for my brother and me, and for my mother too. She had nothing to do with that decision. My father was good with words that way. But like my mother, my brother and I did as we were told. Perhaps my father hoped that we would be safer in Spain from anti-Semitism. So he promised to follow us later. But it turned out differently. We did not know that at the time he was involved with another woman, or that he wanted to move with her from Germany to Holland and live with her in the capital of Amsterdam.

During World War I, to avoid mandatory military service, his parents sent my father to Holland. In 1918, after the war ended, he returned to Berlin. So now in 1932, thanks to his earlier stay, he spoke Dutch.

My father was a resourceful man and very social. He was cheerful, loyal and always ready to help a friend and he had lots of them. He was a solid athlete; an enthusiastic and competitive tennis player. He held his own at competitions. As for work, he had turned his hobbies, cars and movies, into his profession; he imported cars and distributed movies. Business was good and my brother Hans and I wanted for nothing.

My father sold most of our furniture and the like and took some bed linen and silverware from Grandma Lea to Amsterdam. My mother didn't suspect anything and when she found out, she must have been very sad. She never complained though. It must have been hard on her.

But my father did care about our safety and thought the trip to Spain with two children would be safer if my mother traveled on a non-Jewish passport. He figured out a way to lessen the danger during our journey and warned us.

Your mother will be traveling on a fake passport and a different name. Officially she is not your mother during the trip. You must call her aunt Sophie. Remember that. It's important. Don't call her mama.

My father had arranged with Sophie, a close Aryan friend of my mother's, to loan my mother her identity card. With Sophie's identity card, my mother went to a police station and reported her passport lost. Now my mother travelled on a newly issued passport.

So my mother was suddenly 'aunt' Sophie to us on our travels from Düsseldorf to Spain.

Both Hans and I remembered the aunt Sophie secret. The journey on the train was fairly uncomfortable. Hans in particular had a hard time. If my mother forbade him something, he responded with, just you take it easy will you, with your fake passport. My mother chose not to respond. What could she have said?

Once in Spain, Hans and I simply switched from aunt back to mother. That went well and no one asked us about it.

Spain was in turmoil and the Spanish civil war (1936-1939) was looming. The Spanish controlled island of Mallorca, our future home, was not only swarming with Spanish (Nationalist) soldiers, but also refugees. Nazi-Germany and its friend Italy both recognized Spain's General Franco's government and in 1936, nazi-Germany supported General Franco in his attempt to suppress the Republican revolution, by having the Luftwaffe bomb the town of Guernica. Italy supported the Nationalists with thousands of soldiers and volunteers. Franco's nationalist forces would eventually win the civil war from the Republicans.

***

Palma de Mallorca, Spain 1932

The journey by train took us via the coastal city of Barcelona, Spain to the island of Mallorca, an island in the Mediterranean ruled by Spain. My father had asked a friend of his who lived in Barcelona, to meet us at the train station. When the train pulled into the Barcelona station, my mother was thankful that his friend was actually waiting for us on the platform. He drove us to the harbor after we had a bite to eat and saw us off, making sure that we boarded the ship to Palma de Mallorca.

The warm weather was a wonderful welcome. Upon arrival in the harbor of Palma, we were welcomed by volunteers from the Jewish refugees' committee. They took us to our new home; a couple of rooms in a house on *Calle de Bellver*. We called it home for a little over a year. I was nine years old and Hans was ten.

Even though the house had no plumbing or running water, it was a carefree and happy time, at least for my brother and me. Several times a day, Hans and I walked a couple of blocks to a nearby well, to fill four buckets with water. We used a rope over a pulley. It's how we got all our water; for drinking, bathing, laundry and dishes. This small inconvenience could not compete in a million years with the warm weather, the beach and the Mediterranean Sea.

We made friends quickly as kids do and soon we realized that we were not the only Germans on the island. We met actresses Pola Negri and other famous actors on the island. Our neighbor was actress Lolita or 'Lola' Lee.

Pola Negri (1897–1987) was a Polish celebrity and trendsetter who achieved worldwide fame during the silent movies era in Europe and later Hollywood. She was known for her femme fatale roles. Negri's childhood was marked by personal hardship. Her father was sent to Siberia and she was raised by her single mother in poverty. In her teenage years, she suffered tuberculosis. After she recovered, she moved to Warsaw in today's Poland, where she studied ballet and acting. In 1917, she relocated to Germany, where she began appearing in silent films for the Berlin-based UFA studio. She was noticed by Paramount Pictures executives who offered her a $3,000 a week contract. In 1922, she arrived in New York being the first celebrated actor to be imported into Hollywood, setting a precedent for other imported European actors that included Greta Garbo and Marlene Dietrich.

My mother befriended Arthur Segal and his family. Segal was an artist and originally a Romanian Jew who studied in Germany. In 1933, when the nazi-party came to power and because Segal was a Jew, his work was no longer allowed to be exhibited in Germany. Segal decided to leave nazi-Germany and temporarily moved to Palma de Mallorca, while waiting for his immigration papers to England to be sorted. Before leaving with his family for London, my mother modeled for him.

Her portrait turned out beautifully. For my mother especially, it felt good to be in the company of other Germans.

The time we spent in Spain felt truly magical. When I think back, our lives there were wonderful. My brother and I did not have to go to school. I loved swimming and horses and had access to both. Every day, all day long after morning chores, we'd be spending our time on the beach. I befriended local children and picked up Spanish in no time.

Mobilized Spanish soldiers stationed on the island, taught me how to swim. Troops on horseback would haul me up and sit me down in front of them. I enjoyed that to no end. I also had a dog. She was a stray and adopted me. I called her Senta. Senta and I were inseparable. She followed me everywhere. When I got up, she got up. When I sat down, she lay down.

It was an altogether different situation for my mother though. I was unaware of it at the time, but she had the typical problems of an adult and on top of that of a refugee. We had very little money. A refugee committee supported us some and from time to time my father sent us a small amount, but it was barely enough to make ends meet. When money is very tight, every little bit helps. I was unaware about any of this until I was older.

My mother confided in my eleven-year-old brother and he was smart enough to understand. He spoke to the owner of a small shack on the beach that sold coffee, tea and lemonade and told him that he was fluent in German, English and French and that he was looking for a job. He was a cheerful kid and the job earned him quite a few tips, which my mother appreciated a lot. While on the job, he met a friendly German woman. She liked him and asked if he wanted to join her on a trip to the island of Ibiza. She was taking a vacation from her vacation. My mother approved and Hans accompanied her. He had a great time.

My father's absence made my mother sad. All she could do was fill the time with taking walks, and visiting with other German refugees, while waiting in vain for my father to arrive. As for myself, I remember that period as an amazing and unforgettable vacation in the sun.

In Germany the beginning of 1933 was a turning point in history. The nazis so-called power grab meant an end to the Weimar democracy. Jews were openly declared inferior, a blemish to the Aryan race. Throughout Germany they were humiliated in public. Feeling vulnerable, they despaired while their lives were falling apart. Anti-Semitism had become part of the German culture.

***

Amsterdam, Holland 1934

My mother received a letter from her sister Lotte in Cologne, in which she wrote that my father had moved to Holland and was now living in the city of Amsterdam. My mother craved nothing more than for us to live together as a family again and she decided to leave Palma with us and join him in Holland. She sent my father a telegram notifying him that we were on our way to join him. I was devastated and inconsolable when my mother told me that I had to leave Senta behind. She tried comforting me that Senta would find a good home in no time, because she was such a clever dog. I didn't buy it and today I can still feel the pain that I felt then.

In fact, as so often happens in hindsight, we were lucky that my mother decided to pack up and leave, for we were spared the horrific Spanish civil war (1936-1939) that left a path of death and destruction.

Calling my mother aunt Sophie again during the duration of our return trip, the long train ride north through France, Belgium, and part of Holland passed without incident. When we slowly rolled into Amsterdam's Central Station, I saw my father standing on the platform waiting for us. And even though my upbringing was not particularly emotional, I felt quite happy at seeing him. Like my mother, I was hoping to be living again as a regular family. At first we stayed with friends, later we moved into a large rental which my father had arranged through a connection.

To supplement our income, my mother rented out one or two rooms. But even taking in boarders did not improve our money situation.

My grandparents and parents were German. I was born in Germany and when I spoke, I spoke in German. Now I was ten years old and had to attend a transition-type school to first learn Dutch.

My father lived with us for a while, but things between my parents weren't going smoothly. A year after we arrived from Spain, my father moved out and took my brother with him. Fairly soon after their moving out, my father came to visit.

You better go back to Cologne and take Lili with you, he said. Knowing what we found out later, he had his reasons.

There was no discussion. Even though she was deeply unhappy about it, my mother simply did as she was told.

***

Cologne, 1935

In Germany national boycotts against Jewish businesses, law firms and medical practices had started. Jewish owned businesses were forced to close. Signs reading 'Don't buy from Jews' and 'Out with the Jews' were seen all over Germany. Nazi flags were hoisted all over the country. 'Jews not wanted' signs were posted even in the smallest villages.

There was a direct bus service between the cities of Amsterdam and Cologne. My mother had some matters to attend to and I was sent ahead by myself with a suitcase full of clothes and a dead chicken still with its feathers intact. My father dropped me off at the station. Before I got on the bus he said, Make sure when your mother joins you, you are kind to her and do as she says, or I don't know what else to do with you. Our parting wasn't exactly an emotional affair.

Being an eleven-year-old child, I sat next to the driver who was told to keep an eye on me. I was unhappy with this turn of events and longed for Palma, the beach and most of all, I missed my special four-legged friend Senta.

About five hours later, the bus arrived in Cologne. Aunt Klara was waiting for me at the bus station. Aunt Klara was married to my mother's brother Fritz. Her two other brothers had died in World War I.

When aunt Klara told me that grandmother Lea was living with them, it made up for my missing the beach and the warm Spanish weather. I often accompanied her on her walks to the synagogue. My mother's other sister, aunt Lotte and her husband uncle Josef and their children, my cousins Bernard, Ingrid and Ruth lived nearby. They were all older than me and we got on very well. They were warm and welcoming and treated me as one of their own.

At times, I had been a bit jealous of friends who had cozy and steady homes. Now I seemed to have one also.

My aunt enrolled me into the same Jewish school that I had left two years earlier. During my absence, I had fallen far behind. Even though I spoke German, the lesson material sounded like Greek to me. I had a lot of catching up to do.

Attacks on Jews had become the norm across Germany. The new Nuremberg laws declared it illegal for Jews and non-Jews to marry.

In 1936, I began to experience anti-Semitism. After school, teen-agers attending a non-Jewish school in the neighborhood hung out near our school gate waiting for us. When we left the schoolyard, they followed us, taunting us, belting out nazi-propaganda songs.

Jews, filthy Jews! They yelled.

A few weeks after this had become an everyday routine, I checked through the window to see if any boys were hanging about by the gate. If they were, I would wait half an hour or an hour until they left. As time passed by, I became a little more confident. Sometimes I would abruptly turn around, raise my hand to the closest boy near me and pretend to hit him in the face. The cowardly bullies they were, turned around and ran off, laughing and cursing at me as if I had done them wrong. At home, when asked about my day at school, I didn't mention those boys or the insults. No sense in worrying the grownups any more than they already were. No doubt they were experiencing similar ugly matters of concern.

My brother Hans visited every so often, but I was still waiting for my mother who, for various reasons, had not joined me yet. She was still in Holland. In my letters to her, I omitted the commonplace anti-Semitic harassment.

About a year after moving in with uncle Fritz and aunt Klara, I fell ill. The doctor diagnosed diphtheria; a serious infection in my nose and throat that today is easily preventable by getting vaccinated. Uncle Fritz called my mother to let her know that I was sick. She arrived the following day. I was happy to finally see her. She stayed with her sister Lotte and her husband Josef and visited me everyday, nursing me back to life. It took quite a while before I was fully recovered.

I was allowed to join a Zionist social club. At the after-school meetings, I met all sorts of young people my age. Most of them planned on immigrating to Israel. That wasn't necessarily my plan, but I enjoyed spending time with my peers. We studied the Hebrew language and learned Hebrew folk songs. We danced and sang and partied together. When Cologne started to finally feel like home again, I was told that I was moving again. The nazis were in power and the political situation had become too dire to stay. My stay in Cologne lasted two or three years.

Rioting against Jews became more intense. In November 1938, thousands of Jewish homes, businesses and synagogues were vandalized and set ablaze. Thousand Jews lost their lives. That infamous November night is known as the 'night of the broken glass' or 'Crystal Night.'

In 1938, uncle Fritz telephoned my father to tell him that he was taking his family to America. He advised him that given the political climate in Germany, it was safer for me to return to Holland. At her sister Lotte's home, where my mother was staying, the situation became increasingly difficult. Lotte and her husband Joseph weren't sure whether to leave or to stay put until it all blew over. So when uncle Fritz explained to me that I was better off returning to Amsterdam, I didn't mind it a whole lot. It was 1938 and I was now fourteen-years-old when my mother and I packed our bags again. We boarded the bus and returned to Amsterdam together.

Sanctioned government persecution of Jews was in full swing. Jewish businesses were ransacked and ordered closed. Newspaper and radio-bulletins stated anti-Jewish regulations daily. Throughout nazi-Germany signs displaying, 'Don't buy from Jews' sprouted like mushrooms. Everyone we knew was nervous. The lives of German Jews in nazi-Germany came to a standstill.

***

Holland, 1938

My father found us an apartment in a suburb of Amsterdam called Diemen. He brought us beds, some household goods, tableware and a woven mat. He also gave us two sofas that he had brought with him from Germany. We were lucky that he even found us a rental, because living spaces had become hard to come by due to the influx of refugees. Luckily Diemen had a mayor who was willing to take in refugees. The mayor of Amsterdam on the other hand, was pro-nazi.

Hans was living with my father and his girlfriend. This arrangement worked for only so long before Hans came to live with us. The three of us together again felt good. It felt like a real family again. Because I missed Senta so much, my mother found me another dog. I named him Tommie. Not taking politics into account, life seemed pretty good.

This time my mother enrolled me in a Christian school, which made me the only Jewish student in the whole school. I was good at memorizing Bible verses. Always receiving an A+ for delivery. But I had a hard time in class; not because I was Jewish, but because of having fallen behind on the material. I had to learn to read and write Dutch all over again. The teachers didn't think I was capable. So later that year, my mother transferred me to a Jewish high school in the center of Amsterdam. It was quite a long bike ride from where we lived. Fortunately, Hans already attended that school, so we rode our bikes to school together. Most of the students went home for lunch. Hans and I remained at school, eating sandwiches my mother had prepared. Again I made new friends. Like me, many had fled nazi-Germany. Just like in Cologne, where I had enjoyed a sense of belonging, I started to feel at home again. Our cousins Ingrid and Ruth visited from Cologne regularly. We'd take them on day trips, showing them the Dutch tourist locations.

In 1937, my father became a board member of a company called *Film Chemistry*. This company removed silver, lacquer and glue coatings from old feature films. The process was way ahead of its time. Today it's called recycling.

My mother managed to make ends meet with very little money. One evening over dinner, she suggested I should learn a trade. I agreed; I didn't get good grades at school and I found my classes difficult to follow. I was terribly embarrassed when the teacher asked me something in front of the whole class and I didn't know the answer. At least, if I had a profession, I could help my mother out financially. I left school. Hans continued.

I was interested in fashion, so my mother suggested I take evening courses in couture; dressmaking, dress design, tailoring and sewing. While studying, I found work as an intern at a small German outfit that dealt with women's fashion. I earned a little and learned a lot. I was a good student, because I liked what I was learning.

In the spring of 1938, nazi-Germany's troops crossed the border into Austria.

In 1939, I was hired by a woman who owned her own sewing atelier. Several refugees at the atelier had successfully earned a living in Berlin's fashion industry, before escaping to Holland. They treated me with kindness and made me feel comfortable. Customers brought their own fabrics from which we made any design they requested. The days were long. Before I went home, no matter what time, I performed typically beginner's chores like sweeping the floor and cleaning up. I enjoyed working there and I was good at it. I continued attending night classes. When I had a moment for myself, I played tennis or read about fashion. I liked going to the movies with friends or taking long walks with my dog Tommie.

Topics like 'elections,' 'war,' and 'nazis,' were not on the table. Neither with friends, nor at home. Newspaper headlines read *Crystal Night* and you heard about what was going on 'over there in Germany,' but it wasn't in our backyard (yet) and ignorance being bliss was for the young. And I was young. We finally had a cozy home. My brother and I invited friends over. At long last I felt that I belonged. But by now, I knew enough to know that situations could change in a blink of an eye.

***

War, 1940

*September 1, 1939 nazi-Germany invaded Poland.
England declared war on nazi-Germany.*

*May 10, 1940 fell on a Friday. At four o'clock in the
morning, nazi-Germany invaded Holland. The
country's first reaction was one of disbelief. Although
the Dutch government had been informed, they chose
to ignore the warning. After all, Holland had not been
occupied by a foreign power since Napoleon's exit in
1813. By early afternoon, the Third Reich was in
charge of most of Holland's airfields. Four days later,
after the Luftwaffe (the German air force) had
flattened the harbor city of Rotterdam, and wanting to
speed up Holland's surrender, the nazis threatened the
Dutch government with flattening the centrally located
city of Utrecht. The Dutch Commander-in-chief
realized that resisting the enemy was moot and he
decided to surrender. Capitulation papers were signed
the following day. It was May 15, 1940.*

It was an unusually warm night. My bedroom
window stood ajar. Daybreak was around five
o'clock and we were woken up by the sound of
monotonous airplanes humming overhead. The sky
was swarming with planes. I quickly got dressed and
went outside. People were yelling and screaming;
The Germans are here; the Germans are here. It is
war with Germany!

My mother got dressed and joined me outside.
She spoke with the other refugees on our block.

Everyone was in shock. Around seven o'clock that morning, my mother handed me some money and sent me out to buy coffee and sugar. When I got to the store, there was a line already. My mother must have known. Without knowing the word, hoarding had started and this is what it looked like. I was lucky to get there early. At the atelier, my boss and co-workers sent me on a mission to purchase cigars and cigarettes.

A few months into the occupation, my father was removed from his position at *Film Chemistry*, because he was Jewish. However, he managed to make use of his father's Romanian background and obtained papers from the Romanian consulate in Amsterdam. These papers allowed him to continue living in Amsterdam during the war and work as a representative for a company that produced powdered milk. He supported my mother financially and I visited him every month to collect his financial contribution. Beyond that, we didn't have much contact. His support ended when he received an order to report. They wanted him to work in nazi-Germany, to support the war effort.

In the 1920's, while serving a prison term, Hitler wrote a book in which he described the future he had in mind for Germany and its Jews. Some ten years later when he had become Chancellor of Germany, most people thought he was just another nutcase and that all his craziness would pass and things would get back to normal again.

The German Club

Refugees from Germany and Eastern Europe in particular sought each other's company at the Club. In its heyday, the Club hosted various kinds of activities; language courses, inspiring lectures and often times the most passionate and heated political discussions. These refugees comprised single men and women and whole families who came from the most diverse political backgrounds. Some were members of anti-fascist groups in their home country, others were socialist and communist 'brothers' who fought for equal rights, wanting to lessen the gap between the wealthy and the poor. Some believed in the Soviet Union's Communist manifesto. There were heated discussions.

Dutch politicians wanted to remain on nazi-Germany's good side and so it's fair to say that the Dutch government was very unhappy with the influx of all these Jews.

During World War I, German troops on their way to the battlefield in Belgium had the Dutch government's permission to short cut through part of its southern province. In turn Germany promised to observe Holland as a 'neutral' party.

So the time came that the border was closed. Jewish refugees were now stopped at the border and were returned to nazi-Germany. As was well known, this meant they ended up in concentration camps, where they languished and died.

Every Sunday, my mother and I socialized at the Club. We served my mother's very much appreciated home made cheesecake and I volunteered to pour coffee, while listening to the discussions and learning what plans people were making. I didn't participate in the discussions. I simply didn't know enough about it, but I listened and the precarious situation we found ourselves in started dawning on me. Some refugees managed to reach England or America before the invasion. For the rest of us, we found ourselves waking up inside our worst imaginable nightmare. A good conversation, a cup of coffee and a slice of delicious cheese cake were soon to be a thing of the past.

***

The Final Solution

The nazis considered their Dutch neighbors Aryan brothers, so they assured the Dutch politicians that the Dutch people had nothing to worry about. This did not include the Dutch Jews. The Jews from Germany saw the writing on the wall. They knew what life had been like for them in Germany. They had fled to escape the nazi-tentacles, but sadly they had not traveled far enough. Many jumped from windows and balconies to their death. Others ended their lives by turning on the gas in the kitchen stove. Anti-Jewish regulations were announced and months into the occupation, the country was being bombarded with the same anti-Jewish regulations that had been implemented in nazi-Germany and other nazi-occupied countries.

At first new regulations were slowly rolled out. After about six months they were issued in quick succession. Each regulation was more invasive than the next. This continued until our democratic rights were fully eroded and our lives came to a standstill. We were at the mercy of a small group who did not hate us.

It was hard to see the bigger picture. Of course, thinking back to this period with twenty-twenty hindsight, the 'Final Solution' was a mapped out plan. We didn't see it, let alone believe it. Ethnic cleansing on such an organized and systemic industrial scale had never ever happened before.

At first, the general attitude was, as long as it doesn't get any worse, we can handle it.

Like in the other nazi-occupied countries, a Jewish Council was created, compelling Jews to announce the anti-Jewish regulations to fellow Jews. It was a smart scheme to let Jews do the nazis' dirty work. Their logic was that directives coming from the Jewish Council aroused less suspicion. So when a mailman delivered a letter from the Jewish Council with instructions before deportation, you obeyed. The Jewish Council was tasked with picking the families for deportation. When there were no more Jews left, the Council leadership itself, its employees (more than 17.000) and their family members were deported.

***

Registration

A small minority, the politically more astute, decided not to register. Jewish registrants received a black letter 'J' in their identification papers next to their photo. Most people obeyed the registration order for various reasons. Some regarded registration as their duty or feared reprisals. Others did not foresee the consequences of registration. Jewish public servants were fired, while non-Jewish civil servants had to sign a declaration stating they were not Jewish. Protesters were sent to concentration camps from where their death notices started arriving almost immediately. Jews who owned a business had to sell. and received far below market price.

After the mandatory ID distinguished us from the non-Jews, we were ordered to buy and wear the yellow star of David on four layers of clothing. The next phase of the 'Final Solution' was segregation.

Who is a Jew? The German authorities had come up with a formula. A person was considered Jewish when three grandparents were members of a Jewish congregation or married to a member. Persons with two Jewish grandparents were regarded as half-Jews and persons with one Jewish grandparent were considered one quarter Jewish.

***

Nazi Regulations

Plans to eliminate the Jews were organized in phases: segregation, deportation and ultimately elimination. The details were worked out as the war progressed. Bullets proved to be expensive and slow, so scientists, civil engineers and architects came up with something bigger and better, faster and more drastic that had never been implemented before in the history of mankind.

Slowly at first, then more rapidly, the nazi-regime announced new regulations. To segregate or isolate the Jews, the new laws prevented Jews and non-Jews (Aryans) from interacting. To execute phase one, Jews needed to live in one neighborhood. Phase two would then deport them on cattle cars to the concentration camps in "the East." They were going to work is what they were told. What about the elderly, the sick and the too-young to-work? Asking questions got you deported as well.

Here is a small selection of the new regulations:
• Jewish officials, professors, teachers, lecturers were fired.
• Jews had to fire non-Jewish domestic workers.
• Jewish doctors and lawyers were only allowed to have Jewish patients and clients.
• Jews were no longer allowed to visit parks, museums, cafes, restaurants, cinemas, beaches, swimming pools, etc.
• Jews were required to wear the yellow star of David.
• Jews were no longer allowed to marry non-Jews.
• Jews had to sign over their money, securities, antiques, gold and silver items, real estate and all other possessions of value.
• Local, national and international travel was against the law for Jews.
• Shopping was strictly regulated to two hours a day between 3 pm and 5 pm and only in Jewish owned stores.
• Jews were banned from participating in or attending sports events.
• Jews were no longer allowed to use a telephone.
• Jews could no longer visit their non-Jewish friends.
• Deportations letters arrived by ordinary mail. The letter stated exactly what to pack. Pets were to be left behind.

• Jews had to sell their business. They had no choice but to accept whatever amount they were offered.

***

Segregation

The day arrived that we too received the dreaded deportation letter in the mail. It was addressed to my mother. We had three days to get our belongings together and pack for the move to Amsterdam. The instructions read that we could take hand luggage only. Jews who already lived in Amsterdam also received a letter; they were ordered to relocate within the city to a Jewish neighborhood.

The city of Amsterdam benefited enormously from these forced relocations. With the influx of a large number of renters, the rental rates skyrocketed. After a second or sometimes third compelled move, some families decided to go into hiding.

So the day had come that we had to move from a quiet suburb to the bustling (ghetto-like) Jewish quarter in the city of Amsterdam. Finding a living space was my mother's responsibility. In addition to our suitcases, we each carried a backpack. What little household items and furniture we owned, was left behind and got stolen. I had moved often enough to take this move in stride. But I remember thinking that it felt different this time. I was a teenager by now and had made pretty good friends.

This move didn't just feel different; it truly felt like bad news.

On a drizzling evening, at a location not far from where we lived, we boarded a bus with about twenty other families.

The nazis had frozen the Jewish bank accounts and paid for the tram and train fares with monies from the frozen bank accounts to which only they had access. Those deported to concentration camps paid their own one-way fare, and they also paid for the return fares of the guards.

The interior of the bus looked so familiar. It reminded me of happier times. It was the same bus company and probably the exact same bus I rode on many times before; on school outings, day trips, etc. This time it wasn't for pleasure though. Emotionally drained, the adults were silent and only the voices of a few children and a muffled voice of a mother trying to hush her crying baby could be heard. The bus stopped about half an hour later and the driver told us to get off.

It was November. It was cold and drizzling. This was a sinister scene from an even more sinister time in history. Together with my mother and brother, we started our dramatic walk to our new address. With the help of an acquaintance, my mother had found three rooms and a kitchenette on an attic floor we shared with two other Jewish families who had also been forced to move. We walked in silence, almost in a daze, each preoccupied with our own thoughts. We arrived at our new address just after midnight.

German soldiers became a familiar sight everywhere; in the streets, streetcars, trains, in restaurants and theaters, everywhere. At first they could be seen walking by themselves, but some twenty months into the occupation, when the ambiance had turned hostile, they would walk in pairs or small groups of three or more.

These were difficult times. Rights we took for granted were being stripped away; right to work, study, travel, move, socialize, etc. Imagine receiving a letter that orders you and your family to move. Even if you were not religious, but your grandparents were. Life became unbearable and impossible.

Going into hiding brought a whole different set of problems with it. First you had to find a place. You needed a trustworthy person to lead you to a dependable host family. Hiding was expensive. Many hosts offered hiding places only for the extra income. Often times when money ran out, which it invariably did, because bank accounts were frozen, the host informed the police and so made a few bucks at the end of the deal. Another issue was the neighbors. If before the invasion neighbors had been friendly, during the war many ratted on each other.

If the host family was ratted on, they could be imprisoned or sent to a concentration camp. If the host family had children, they were trained not to talk to friends at school about their new 'guests.'

If several immediate family members or even different families hiding at the same location did not get along, their arguments could put them at risk of getting caught.

In May of 1942, wearing the yellow star of David on three layers of clothing became mandatory. The cotton star had to be stitched on. Pinning it on made it too easy to remove and was therefore illegal. Regulations concerning the Jewish population were published in a weekly newspaper published by the Jewish Council. Some non-Jews showed solidarity and protested by also wearing a star, but this was quickly squashed by threats of imprisonment and even deportation to a concentration camp.

My mother returned home from a visit to the office of the Jewish Council. She had bought nine yellow stars. We each got three. One for a winter coat, one for a summer jacket and the third one for an in-between seasons sweater. My mom asked me to sew them on. There was a penalty for not wearing the yellow star at all, or for wearing it in the wrong place. The inside joke was that the star of David needed to be worn on the left hand side of the chest, over the heart. It felt awful walking in public with that yellow star showing. Not that I minded being Jewish, but I didn't want to stand out. Some people nodded with empathy, others made nasty comments under their breath or even openly cursed at you; dirty Jew or you finally get what you deserve.

***

Deportations

The orders to report for mandatory labor were delivered by regular mail. You had three days to report. Some time later the occupier felt that the mail service was too slow and police men would drop the letter off through the mail slot. When that took too long, policemen started showing up at the registered addresses, close to midnight, when they knew that the families were home, asleep. Later still they were taken away in broad daylight. If the front door wasn't opened fast enough, the men would kick the door down. The sick and the elderly were dragged out of bed, into the street in their pajamas. Army trucks were lined up in the neighborhood, ready to transport the families to a holding facility, from where they were taken to camp Westerbork. Concentration camp Westerbork was a horrible camp, but at least it was still in Holland. This gave the doomed prisoners some hope that things could still change in their favor. This scheme to eliminate a whole group of people because of their race or religion, (today we call it genocide) was quite methodically executed.

***

1942

Razzia's (police raids, whereby anyone wearing a yellow Star of David was picked up from home or stopped in the street and forced into the back of an army truck), were in full swing. In the process of hunting down Jews, the German Grüne Polizei worked together with the Dutch police force and various Dutch civil services. By the third quarter of 1943, more than 93,000 Jews had been deported, a figure that rose to about 107,000 a year later.

One balmy summer evening while walking home down a quiet neighborhood street, I found myself suddenly caught up in the middle of a major police raid. From both directions several canvas-covered army trucks followed by police cars turned the corner into the street and screeched to a halt. They parked diagonally to stop traffic. The *Grüne* policemen jumped out from the back of the trucks, while the Dutch policemen rerouted traffic. A man wearing civilian clothing seemed to be in charge and shouted out street numbers from a list. The *Grüne* men ran to the numbered front doors and started banging the doors. All this went on accompanied by the policemen yelling and shouting for the family members to hurry up and dogs aggressively barking. If a person didn't move fast enough, they were hit and kicked towards the waiting trucks. Elderly in their pajama's were dragged out of bed and ordered into the back of the waiting trucks. Crying children were picked up and thrown into the back of the trucks. Pedestrians wearing a yellow Star of David who happened to be walking there were apprehended and also put in the back of the waiting trucks.

I watched all this and froze. I didn't know what to do. All of a sudden, I felt an arm under my elbow and saw a man's big fist covering my yellow star of David. The man whispered into my ear, asking where I lived. I told him. He turned me and said in a loud voice pointing up, see that flowerpot on the balcony up there, that's where I live. I looked where he was pointing and at that same moment, out of the corner of my eye, I saw soldiers and policemen running by us towards a couple walking towards us. The man at my arm said, I am walking you home. Don't worry.

My mother and my brother heard the noise down in the street and watched from the fourth floor attic window. They were frantic, because I had not gotten home yet. Suddenly they saw me walking up with a stranger whose fist covered my star. My anonymous rescuer whispered into my ear that I should go to the regional employment office and ask for Mr. Hansen. He shook my hand and said, well now, better get inside. Best of luck. I thanked him and he was gone. I was saved by a complete stranger. I don't ever want to go though this again, I thought to myself as I climbed the steep stair case to the attic floor. I never saw my anonymous protector again. I made a point of remembering Mr. Hansen's name and committed it to memory.

Then it was our turn. My mother received the dreaded letter. We were called up to report for mandatory labor in the East. But I wondered. Why are babies and grandparents called up for work? My mother had a cousin who worked for the Jewish Council. She went to ask him for advice. He just said that it was best that we pack our bags and report at the train station at the designated time.

***

Exemptions

When my mother came home with her cousin's advice, I flat out refused. I was firm. I wouldn't budge. That was the first time I did not obey. Putting my foot down I added that I was removing the star from all my clothing. I told her and my brother not to leave the house unless they absolutely had to. At that time, I was studying for my sewing and design finals and was determined to pass. Getting my diploma was very important to me. The stress of it all got to me and I decided to stop working and concentrate on studying only.

The Sperr stamp in an ID was a coveted stamp that offered a (temporary) exemption from deportation. If issued a Sperr, you were designated indispensable at work. New regulations were being published on a weekly basis; The Dutch Cinema Association refused Jews access to its theaters. Jewish teachers, professors and

Jews in the public sector had been fired. Public swimming pools and beaches were off limits. Signs posting 'No Jews Allowed' were now a regular sight in parks, zoos, restaurants, cafes, hotels, cinemas, libraries, museums, etc. Jewish attorneys, pharmacists and doctors were no longer allowed to consult, sell to or treat non-Jewish clients, customers or patients. Access to the stock exchange was now prohibited.

I passed my sewing and design finals. Now that I had a skill, I had a reason to go to the regional employment office and find Mr. Hansen. My problem was that I was a stateless foreigner. Germany had rescinded my passport. So I didn't have the proper paperwork to get a work permit. Perhaps Mr. Hansen could help me. Hans Hansen sat behind the counter at the regional employment office. He was a just man. His kindness and willingness to take risks knew no bounds. He took notes while asking all kinds of questions about me and my family. About half an hour later he told me that he'd do his best to help me find work and he would be in touch. I thanked him, got up and walked towards the exit. He caught up with me in the lobby and said with a loud voice that I had forgotten my newspaper. While handing me a paper, he whispered a street address and time for us to meet the following day.

As I arrived, I watched him approach by foot. He was holding the hand of a little girl; she was maybe 5 years old. During our walk he asked about my plans. I had none. Except for one. To prevent my mother, brother and me from being deported. I needed to find work in order to get *a Sperr stamp.*

Mr. Hansen said that if I wanted to work, I needed a work permit and to get that I needed a new ID without the 'J' stamp. At the end of the conversation he gave me instructions, told me to remember them and not to write any of it down. He told me the address of a police station and the name of a police officer. Tell him that you lost your ID and that you need to apply for a new one. I shouldn't say anything more than that. In regards to work, Mr. Hansen suggested that I report to the Sewing Office of the Jewish Council. He would call them, so they'd be expecting me. His last piece of advice was that I color my hair. I blindly trusted Mr. Hansen. Just went with my gut.

The Sewing and Mending office acted as the distribution point for clothing, backpacks and blankets for Jews who were about to be deported. They also mended Wehrmacht uniforms.

The following morning, I looked at my image in the mirror. What I saw looked right from an advertisement for the Aryan race baby-breeding program known as *Lebensborn.* Blonde suited me. First thing that morning, I went to have passport size photos taken and afterwards I went to the police station.

In the busy lobby I asked for the police officer whose name I had memorized. I was shown to his desk. The officer motioned me to sit down in the

49

chair across from his desk. He needed a moment to finish paperwork for the person he'd seen before me. I scanned the room and noticed a little swastika flag on every desk. When he was done he looked up and smiled at me. How could he help me? I repeated exactly the words Mr. Hansen had told me to say. No more, no less. The officer told me not to worry and that I had come to the right place. He gave me several forms to fill out and when I was done, I handed him the forms back with my new passport size photos. I would get a letter in the mail when my ID was ready for pick up. In all, it took no longer than thirty minutes. I felt my heart pounding as I left the police station.

I was pumped. The hope that this could postpone or even cancel our deportation, calmed me down somewhat. But I knew I wasn't out of the woods yet. As I walked home, I decided that I wasn't ready to tell my mother or brother about this yet. Also, I needed to find someone to go with me when my new ID was ready for pick up. What if something went wrong. My mother and brother won't know where to start looking for me.

The Sewing Office of the Jewish Council was a couple of doors down from the German club where I used to visit with my mother on Sundays. The office made a chaotic impression. There were six of us. We mended everything from backpacks to blankets, clothing, socks, etc. for the families who were about to be deported. We also repaired uniforms for the *Wehrmacht*. I guess the Jewish

Council wanted to try and stay on their good side. We tried to be upbeat. Behind the optimistic façade, we were concerned and restless. Work felt two fold. I realized that the person who was going to be wearing the coat I was repairing, was not going on a fun summer vacation trip. But we never imagined that they'd be dead a couple of days later. The general attitude of those in their 40's and younger was: we are young, we are healthy, we can work. Of course, mending *Wehrmacht* uniforms felt strange. It kept us from being deported because we were needed, but we were indirectly working for the enemy.

A few weeks went by. Then a letter arrived from the Citizen's Registration office. My new identity card was ready for pick up. I contacted Mr. Hansen for instructions. I should ask for Mr. Landweer, the office supervisor. Mr. Landweer was another hero. Later I heard that he had retrieved my old identity card with the dreaded 'J' and replaced it with a copy of a new card without a 'J.'

***

Fake Papers

Leo Weil was part of the same close-knit circle of friends as my brother. All five or six of them had roots in Germany. Leo was a few years older than me. When I ran into him one late afternoon, he insisted on walking me home. When I told him what I had done and that I didn't want to pick up my ID by myself, he immediately offered to go with me. Leo was not averse to putting his life on the line for the cause. The cause was defeating and kicking the nazis out by any means necessary. He traveled with fake documents using a fake name, unlike me; my fake papers listed my real info.

Many fake documents showed names of someone who was dead. In the chaos this went unnoticed.

Leo suggested to go at a time when it was at its busiest. He was going to follow me at a distance and in case of trouble, he told me to exit the building and not react or look up at anyone calling my name or ordering me to stop. Leo owned a gun and assured me that he had my back. Stay focused and walk out the building.

The next day was a typically gloomy drab overcast morning. Leo's long leather coat and hat made him look like he worked for the secret police. He kept his distance.

It was fairly hectic inside the hall of the Citizen's Registration office. Some lines had already formed in front of the teller-like stations. My eyes scanned the wooden name plates and my trepidation dissipated somewhat when I saw the station with Mr. Landweer's name plate. I walked over and stood in line. Where is Leo? I kept eyeing the entrance as the line I was waiting in shortened. Just before it was my turn to step up to the window, Leo entered holding a newspaper. He found a seat in the busy waiting area. I stepped up to the window and told Mr. Landweer my name and my reason for being there. I had come to pick up my ID. I gave him the letter. Mr. Landweer nodded, got up and disappeared. I could hardly breathe. From the corner of my eye I could see Leo looking my way over the edge of his open newspaper. After a few minutes which felt forever, Mr. Landweer reappeared. He was holding a file with my paperwork. He looked through the file and seemed to double check a few things. He had me sign a receipt and when he handed me my new ID, he wished me good luck adding that I should be careful not to lose it again. I thanked him, turned around and left the building.

When Leo caught up with me a couple of streets over, he nodded silently and smiled. The sun had come out from behind the clouds and the morning felt less gloomy. I felt as if I had regained my freedom. Of course it wasn't like that at all. Danger waited around every corner. Leo asked if I had noticed the other secret policemen in the waiting room area. I was glad that I hadn't.

With my ID looking 'legal,' my next stop was Mr. Hansen at the employment office. I wanted to work. If I worked, I didn't have to hide indoors 24/7. Outside, I had to stay alert, but at least I could move about. My new ID card showed I was born in Germany, which was true. The rest of the information was also accurate. Being able to answer truthfully meant that I didn't have to memorize a made up biography. The only but major difference was that I was now registered as an Aryan, instead of a Jew.

When I came home, I showed my mother and brother my new ID. I was going to try and do the same for them. My mother wasn't sure. What if I got caught? Through my contacts, I got my mother a new identity card and for Hans, we managed to get him a new passport. I reported my ID missing at several police stations throughout the country.

The quality of communication between the various agencies was weak and streamlining lots of paperwork within the different departments of the many agencies took months if not years. With help from connections in the resistance, my photo and name were expertly replaced with the new bearer's info.

Despite her new ID, my mother felt it was unsafe to go out and throughout the war she remained mostly indoors. After the three of us had new ID's, I started helping friends who were in hiding. Thanks to the willingness to put their own lives on the line, Mr. Landweer and Mr. Hansen saved many lives. Unfortunately, one day Landweer was betrayed by a co-worker. He was arrested and swiftly executed. I came across others who were brave and willing to fight the nazi-tyrant. Mr. Onderwijzer risked his life by providing me with food vouchers. Another contact had access to blank passports. Landweer, Hansen and Onderwijzer never asked for money.

Fighting the nazis was so intensely dangerous, because their justice system knew no extenuating circumstances. Being caught meant certain death; either by execution or by deportation to a concentration camp, where you would surely die.

As time went by, the round ups became relentless. Banging on doors shifted flagrantly from night time to day time. Anyone walking outside and wearing a star was also picked up. Sperr stamp or no Sperr stamp in their ID. By the end of 1944, when most of the Jews were gone, the bureaucrats responsible for keeping the deportation lists and the general paper mill up to date, got sloppy.

From the skylight in the typical Dutch slanted red-tiled roof, we watched how Dutch police men pulled entire families into the street; pushing fathers and mothers and their children into the back of waiting army trucks. A pet dog followed the family into the street. Confused by the noise of the yelling police men and their barking dogs, the pet dog barked at the aggressively barking police dogs. One of the officers cursed at the dog and kicked the poor thing mercilessly back into the house. My eyes teared up as I remembered Senta, my beloved and loyal playmate in Spain that had shown me so much love and devotion.

Then our first floor neighbors' door bell rang. Impatiently, it rang a bunch of times. It was followed by banging. Open up and come out side, voices yelled. We heard the front door being kicked in. The floor below us was rented to a German

55

woman whose son served in the *Wehrmacht* and happened to be on furlough, visiting his mom. He had just arrived from the front and he happened to be at his mom's when the raid took place. He heard the noise of the soldiers pounding on the front door and he didn't like it. The ground floor neighbors took their time to open. As they were dragged out into the street, more soldiers entered through the front door and made their way up the narrow staircase. All that noise must've annoyed the visiting son. He opened the front door of his mother's apartment still wearing his *Wehrmacht* uniform. Standing in the doorway to the stairwell, we heard him yell at the soldiers for making a ruckus. They apologized and continued their way up to the attic, to us. Then we heard the son yell at them that there are no Jews here and they must leave. The soldiers didn't argue. They turned around and went down the staircase. Three extended families with numerous children, cousins, nieces and nephews were deported from our address downstairs that day.

I went back to the skylight. The neighbor's front door was taped off to restrict entry. The unfortunate dog sat in the window for days, waiting in vain for its owner to return. Several days later the dog was gone from the window. I told my mother that I very much hoped that someone had rescued it.

After numerous discussions, we decided not to respond to the neatly typed letter addressed to my mother. It had arrived in the mail, ordering my mother to report with her two children for deportation. It was time for us to split up and go into hiding. The neighborhood had become too dangerous. I was determined to move us. I told my mother that I was going to find three different addresses for each of us.

Every so often, I got stopped by the police for a routine ID check. Because I sounded German and my papers stated I worked for the *Wehrmacht,* they didn't suspect me of being anything else than what my ID showed. I looked and spoke the part.

***

Fritz

My brother Hans and Fritz met at the German club and they became friends. Fritz and his parents had come to Holland from Düsseldorf, a small town in Germany close to the Dutch border. His father wanted to get away from the nazis and moved his family across the border. The nazis didn't allow the Jews fleeing Germany to take anything with them, so Fritz's dad had to set up a new business from scratch.

I had noticed Fritz at the German club. He was a couple of years older than me and barely noticed me. He was handsome and smart. He was the type of person men and women were drawn to. He usually could be found with a group of his peers fiercely discussing politics over a cup of coffee and a piece of my mom's cheesecake which he loved. At this time, when the Jews were ordered to move to Amsterdam, his parents decided that it was time to go into hiding. They disappeared to a farm in the north east of the country.

Fritz was a don't-tell-me-what-to-do kind of guy. Hiding was not for Fritz. He wanted to fight the nazis. Refusing to wear the yellow star, he relocated from the southern border town of Maastricht to the capital city of Amsterdam.

Hans only brought friends home he trusted with his life. So one day Hans brought Fritz home. I was not the only one who thought he was handsome, smart and funny. He visited Hans sporadically, but then he started coming around more often. If Hans wasn't home, he would wait for him and we'd talk for hours. Or, he talked and I listened, learning about all kind of things, but mostly politics, the tricky power games.

Fritz had a gift. He was confident and didn't panic. He could talk his way out of anything. And he did. He was a natural. I liked him; his way of thinking, his insight. His wit made me smile. His ideas were fascinating. He was convinced that the nazis would lose this war. He was an educated and well-read German and understood the nature of nazi-ideology; it was built on hate. That could not last. The thousand-year *Reich* won't last five, is what he used to say.

Hans, Leo and Fritz were in the resistance. They trusted each other. They had each other's back. Trust is *the* most valuable currency during a war. Who you trust was a matter of life and death.

Fritz knew from Leo about my fake ID without the 'J' stamp. Leo had also told him that I was helping others. Fritz and I started spending time together, helping each other help others. He had his connections and I had mine. Fritz, Hans and Leo. The three of them fought the nazi-regime and assisted where help was needed. Sometimes it was helping people escape across the Dutch border into Belgium.

Belgium and France were also occupied by the nazis. From Belgium there was an escape route to France, from where one could continue on to Spain or Switzerland. Both choices were inherently risky. Many people were stopped and arrested en route and ended up in a concentration camp.

During World War I and World War II to ensure fair distribution of food during times of shortages, the government issued distribution cards with coupons or vouchers. This voucher system ensured that all kinds of food and other basic goods were available to every one, in exchange for a coupon. It was the government way of preventing people from stocking up. There was a huge black market in distribution cards and vouchers. The newspapers announced what vouchers were redeemable on what days and for what products. A few years into the war, there were long queues everywhere. People always needed vouchers. If you had money, but no coupons, you were in trouble. Booklets and vouchers were personally linked; that is, to one individual only. This made securing food for people in hiding very difficult. Once in a while members of the resistance organized a raid on a distribution office to get their hands on as many blank ID cards as possible. The nazis usually retaliated by executing civilians; mothers, children grandparents.

Fritz and Leo had a contact called Frans. Frans published illegal pamphlets. He wanted to try to reach Switzerland via France. The day before their departure, Leo, Fritz and Frans and I were walking on our way to a clandestine meeting, not far from where we lived. As usual we carried our fake documents on us. In addition, Leo and Fritz carried letters (written, stamped and signed by Hans, stating that the holders of these letters were on 'Government Business.'

Across the street, two *Gestapo* men exited a small neighborhood convenience store. They were talking and walked our direction. We noticed them before they noticed us. We couldn't hear what *Gestapo* man 1 said to *Gestapo* man 2, but they crossed the street over to our side, now walking straight at us. When they reached us, they obstructed our way. So what have we got here, the one in charge asked his mate in German. He studied our faces and turned to me.

You're all Jews, aren't you?

We are Germans, I replied in German, not Jewish.

We get that a lot, Fritz added in German.

Gestapo man 1 asked for my papers, while *Gestapo* man 2 asked Fritz where we were headed. Fritz produced his 'Government Business' letter and handed it to him.

We are on our way to a meeting.

While *Gestapo* man 2 kept questioning Fritz, his mate studied my ID for the longest moment, before handing it back to me. Fritz turned to me and said, you better let them know that we are running late. He looked at *Gestapo* man 1 to see if he would let me leave. But I didn't want to seem too eager by rushing off quickly.

Gestapo man 2 handed Fritz the letter back, wished us a good day and we continued on our way.

***

The Farmer's Wife

Fritz needed to drop off food vouchers at a farmhouse, where a farmer was hiding Jews on his property. Fritz asked me to go with him. The train ride north would take a couple of hours.

Train rides were a tense business in those days. There was a network of surveillance on public transportation. Plain clothed *Gestapo* and Dutch detective or Jew tracing units were plentiful. They worked in pairs. They stopped and searched at will and if they sensed something was off, they had the right to take you in for questioning.

If you got detained on a train, you were trapped. There was nowhere to go. Jumping off as watched in the movies, when the jumper rolls over, gets up and runs away unharmed is unlikely.

Fritz decided to take a chance one busy morning during rush hour, when people were going to work. We arranged a time in front of the train station. There was a slight drizzle going as I walked the one-hour walk to Amsterdam Central Station. That day I may have been early or Fritz was late. By now, I knew enough not to hang about or I'd be noticed. Not wanting to linger in front of the station, I continued walking as if I were on my way to somewhere else. Around the corner, I turned around and walked back. After having done so three or four times, I wondered how much longer I should wait. Had something happened to him? Had he been arrested? Should I wait or should I leave? All kinds of different scenarios went through my head. Just as I decided to wait a few more minutes, I felt a hand grabbing my shoulder. I turned around and there I stood facing a short man dressed in a long black leather coat. His stature didn't intimidate me, but his voice did. A 5'1" bald Dutch policeman with bad teeth ordered me to follow him. I believed that he had something else in mind than taking me to the police station.

Prepare all you like for a moment like this, but when your heart pumps so hard that your chest feels it's about to explode, you freeze. I had to stall him. I didn't follow him. Instead, while looking for my ID in my purse, I told him that I worked for the *Wehrmacht*. He looked at my ID.

What are you doing here? Near the station? he asked. I answered that I had the day off and I was waiting to meet my boyfriend. But he was always late, I complained. I have been waiting for at least fifteen minutes and I am furious. I am done with him for good. His look went from my face to my identity card and back to my face. My German accent in Dutch was undeniable. His posture relaxed and he took a milder tone. He handed me my identity card back.

Ok miss, you can go. He shouldn't keep a pretty girl like you waiting.
I turned around and started walking away. But I knew that he kept watching me. Then I saw Fritz walking towards me.

Keep walking. I'm being watched, I whispered when he was within earshot.

I turned the corner and entered the station building through a side entrance. Fritz walked right by the policeman, wished him good morning and entered through the main entrance. On the platform we kept our distance. When the train arrived, he boarded a different compartment. After the train left the station, he slowly made his way towards me. We avoided looking at each other. Your life really hung by a thread. It could go wrong at any moment. One glance could get you arrested and killed. Louis Malle's movie *Bonjours les Enfants* or *Goodbye children* is about exactly that. One glance.

We separately got off the train and separately exited the station. He took his time catching up with me. The police had stopped him on his way to meeting me at the train station. That's why he was late. They wanted to interrogate him at the police station, but he talked them out of it. While walking from the train station to the farm, he told me that he had brought his parents to this farm only a few months ago and that he had not seen them since. I worried about my mother. Perhaps they could accommodate her there too?

In the countryside at the start of the occupation, the situation was a bit more relaxed than in the city, but in the small villages everyone knew each other's business and this business of hiding Jews openly was not going to end well. A recipe for disaster.

A few weeks later on another typical dreary morning, Fritz and I accompanied my mother to her new hiding place. Her suitcase may have aroused suspicion. While waiting on the platform for the train, two security police officers approached us demanding to see our papers. One of them was German. Fritz answered the usual questions.

Going on vacation?

The Dutch officer asked motioning to the suitcase Fritz was carrying for my mom. Fritz explained that we were taking my mother to her sister who was dying. She was going to stay with her for a few days.

While the Dutch officer checked our papers, Fritz chatted with the German officer about Hitler's favorite soccer club. Germany's *Schalke 04* had just defeated *Vienna FC* during the soccer championships. After more soccer talk the two of them kindly wished us a pleasant day.

The three-hour train ride passed without incident. But this time when we arrived at the farm, it was around noon time, we were in for a proper shock. We entered a lively, smoke-filled living room with people socializing over a cup of coffee. The farmer's wife welcomed us as if she was welcoming us to a party and as if dropping off my mother was a happy occasion.

For the farmer and his wife, it probably was. Financially they gained a lot. They weren't only paid in cash, they also received food vouchers, jewelry, clothes and other valuables.

On our previous visit, the farmer seemed gruff and preferred silence over small talk. His wife had not been home, so I had not formed an impression of her. This time she was home. Her manner was over the top exuberant. She turned out to be a real chatter box. There was nothing discreet about her. In a room full of people, she asked us if traveling without a yellow Star caused us anxiety.

When we talked in private with Fritz's parents, we got a clearer picture. The farmer's wife lacked all forms of integrity. Instead of staying under the radar, the farmer's wife regularly invited village folks over in the morning for a cup of coffee and in the afternoon for a *jenevertje* or a Dutch gin, a hard liquor made from juniper berries.

The farmhands go about their business, but they must be aware of the goings on in the main house, Fritz's father said. We don't feel safe here. We spend most of the time in a bedroom we share with another Jewish family.

When Fritz's father mentioned something to the farmer, he answered that he was free to leave. No one kept him there against his will.

It was clear that this situation was untenable. Fritz agreed that we needed to move his parents and my mother out of there as soon as possible. Every so often Fritz and I took a trip over there and every visit, we encountered social interactions with people visiting from the village. It was only a matter of time until things would go terribly wrong.

Dutch citizens in certain professions received permission to keep their bikes, everybody else had to

66

*turn theirs in. Germans were allowed to keep theirs.
Theirs being the bikes they had confiscated, read stolen
from the Dutch.*

Before I got my brother his new ID, my goal was
finding a place for him to hide. For several weeks I
rode my bike around Amsterdam looking for
window signs advertising 'Rooms to Let.'

In the southern part of the city, not far from the
city center, I looked in the window of a typical
Dutch kiosk, one that sells cigarettes, cigars,
tobacco, rolling paper, magazines, newspapers and
sweets, etc. It also had a rental display list.

There were plenty of vacancies. Lots of people
had fled the city. Not only the Jews. Able men of
drafting age also tried to escape their fate. I wrote a
number of addresses down and went hunting. I
studied each address in detail; I observed the
neighborhood, who entered and exited the front
door. I tried to get info on the owners; were they
patriotic, what kind of ideology did they adhere to,
were they nazi-collaborators, who were the other
tenants in the building, neighbors on the same floor,
etc. When I decided that a room or entire floor was
worthwhile checking out, I concentrated on the lay
out of the building, the apartment floor plan and
escape exits. I favored attic floors. Connecting roofs
to adjoining buildings were potential escape routes.

I had learned from the unfortunate situation my
mother was in and felt terribly responsible. If
something happened to either of them, I'd never be

able to forgive myself. But, at the same time my gut told me that the neighborhood where Hans and I were living now, surely meant deportation.

In 1943, the nazis instructed all men between the ages of 18 and 35 to report to the employment offices. They were to be sent to Germany. Exemptions would be granted only to those whose profession made them indispensable. Healthy men were rounded up and enlisted to work (forced labor) and contribute to the German war effort. Many were sent to the eastern front, where they died fighting the Soviets.

***

Hide

After about ten days of walking and riding by the same address, I decided to ring a bell; the Pollman family had a six-year-old son. According to the ad, they had an attic room for rent. I told Mr. Pollman that I was looking for a room for my brother.

We live in Rotterdam and he is a student.

I told them his age group was being sent to Germany and because we don't really know what goes on over there, my mother wasn't keen.

By expressing myself in a certain way and using certain words, in a certain tone of voice, I hoped to be able to tell if Mr. Pollman was a friend or a foe, trustworthy or nazi-collaborator.

Mr. Pollman answered decisively.

He may come and live with us, as long as he is not a nazi-sympathizer.

He could have been fishing, but I sensed he was sincere.

The roof leaked and water seeped down the wall. But I kept my mouth shut. I had found a hiding place for my brother at last. I gave Hans the address and told him to go there first thing in the morning.

***

Frau Griezell

Now I needed to find a hiding place for myself. I returned to the tobacco kiosk with the rental ads, hoping to find a room close to where my brother was staying. I studied the advertisements, read them countless times and visited many rooms.

In a residential neighborhood, on a quiet street, a young German woman opened the front door.

I came for the rental, I told her in Dutch.

She apologized and said she was German and didn't understand Dutch. She was thrilled that I switched to German and even more so when I told her that I was German too. I told her that I lived and worked in Rotterdam, but that my work had transferred me to Amsterdam.

Over a cup of coffee Frau Griezell told me that she had a boy and a girl and she and her two small children lived on the ground floor. Her Dutch husband worked as a captain for a commercial shipping company. At this time, he was stuck in the

United States unable to return to Holland due to the war. Frau Griezell worked at a *Wehrmacht* office in Amsterdam. I think she supervised cleaning crews. Alarm bells went off in my head. How will that affect me? Will I be safe here?

And what do you do? I heard her ask.

I told her that I also worked for the *Wehrmacht*, but that the project I was currently working on was classified. I apologized that I couldn't really share more about my work with her. She nodded that she understood. She seemed to want to bond with me and I wasn't sure if that was a good thing.

She was looking to rent out all three rooms on the second floor. It included a kitchenette and a bathroom. She showed it to me. It was clean and neat. She adjusted the rent because I was German and because she really wanted me to move in. I found the location ideal. This woman was friendly, but I worried about her connection to the *Wehrmacht*. I told her that I liked it a lot. I was probably interested in renting all three rooms, seeing that I expected colleagues from Rotterdam to stay over from time to time. Wanting to check with Hans and Fritz, I told her that I'd get back to her later that day or the following morning.

I cycled to Hans in a hurry. Luckily Fritz was visiting. We discussed the idea of me moving in first and they would move in shortly after. Hans commented that we'd be living in the lion's den. So here I was, a Jewish woman renting a floor from what soon proved to be a fiercely anti-Semitic German Reich nazi, still it felt good to leave that terrifying neighborhood behind with its hellish round ups.

When Frau Griezell met Hans and Fritz, she immediately liked both of them. She liked funny and smart men, she commented to me afterwards. Hans told Frau Griezell that he and Fritz worked for the *Gestapo*, but at this time they were loaned out to the *Sicherheitsdienst*. He emphasized that she should keep this to herself. Since we all spoke high German and pretended to be German nazis, she believed us without any suspicion. It turned out that she was an uneducated woman and a ferociously Jew hating nazi. My stomach turned every time she ranted against the Jews. She always talked about *Die Scheiss-Juden*, or "those shit Jews." Not to worry Frau Griezell, soon enough not a single *Scheiss-Jude* will be left alive in Holland. Our *Führer* will take care of that, Fritz encouraged her.

I often thought, if she only knew. But fortunately, Frau Griezell fell for our stories, hook, line and sinker. A few days after moving in, Fritz and I got engaged. I asked Frau Griezell if she was okay with Fritz and Hans moving in. There was plenty of space on my floor. She didn't mind one bit. In fact, she liked the idea of having a couple of *Gestapo* men living in her house.

It makes me feel safe, you know.
I didn't know what she meant at the time, but I didn't react. Later we found out that she sold hard liquor on the black market.

It goes without saying that Frau Griezell told her friends at work about the three respectable tenants that rented her second floor.

They are Germans. The two men work for the *Gestapo* and the woman works for the *Wehrmacht*. She repeated every lie we fed her, as we hoped she would.

Hans told Mr. Pollman that he was moving out. He trusted his landlord by now. He told him that he was Jewish and asked him if our mother could move in. Hans felt that Mr. Pollman had a right to know, because as a landlord renting to a Jew, he was endangering himself and his family. If a suspicious neighbor notified the police, they wouldn't believe Mr. Pollman's excuse that he hadn't known.

Pollman didn't have a problem with my mother moving in. Hans and I were over the moon. My mother could finally move away from the farm.

It must have been 1943 or 1944. About six months had gone by since Fritz and Hans had moved in with me on the second floor in the pleasantly quiet residential neighborhood of Amsterdam's south side. The south side was considered a middle class neighborhood. Most husbands could be seen leaving for work in the morning and returning late afternoon.

Sometimes there were nine of us staying at Frau Griezell's second floor; Hans's girlfriend Barbara, Leo Weil and a married couple. All Germans and all

Jewish. We told Frau Griezell that they were on vacation visiting from Germany.

At times when Leo stayed with us, I helped him with his activities. Leo had connections with members of various resistance groups. With the help of a connection, he traveled to north western France, where he got himself hired in a factory in the town of Abbeville on the river Somme. The factory's main customer was the *Wehrmacht*. A *Wehrmacht* liaison associate had a desk inside the factory's administration office.

Leo used his time at the factory to befriend certain female employees at the administration office. It took him a few months to get familiar with the layout of the office, storage and supply rooms and the schedules of the office personnel. One day during lunch time while the office was unattended, Leo entered the supply room and helped himself to a stack of stationery. After lunch he reported sick and traveled back to Amsterdam.

The stationery Leo brought back was used to obtain various official documents; travel and curfew exemptions and 'Government Business' purposes.

Everything about traveling was dangerous. The clothes you wore, the suitcase, bag or purse you carried, the company you were in; for the secret police these were all clues. One wrong word or one untimely stare could endanger not only you, but also your contacts. Each country required a different set of travel documents issued in its own language. Companies or businesses with pro-nazi management were likely to get certain

*employees travel documents, no matter what country.
To make forged documents look official, Fritz and
Hans used original stamps stolen at work by one of our
contacts.*

I was eighteen or nineteen years old by now. Frau
Griezell was only a few years older; she must have
been no more than twenty-three, twenty-four years
old. Soon after I moved in, she insisted that we drop
the polite or formal German pronoun *Sie* (for you)
and use the more informal *Du* instead. So the first
Saturday morning after I had moved in, Frau
Griezell invited me to come downstairs and have a
cup of coffee with her. She told me again that her
husband piloted cargo ships. He got stuck in the
United States when the war broke out.

*Patrolling the Atlantic Ocean, nazi U-boats
(Unterseeboot) mercilessly terrorized and sank many
allied ships. At one time during the war, their U-boats
made it really close to Long Island, NY.*

In addition to a husband overseas, Frau Griezell
had a German lover who visited her in Amsterdam.
Richardt was a German soldier who loved to
surprise her by unexpectedly turning up on her
doorstep. One evening she stood at the bottom of
the stairwell when we heard her impatiently calling
first my name. When I didn't react fast enough, she
called out for Fritz and Hans.

Come down please. I want you to meet a friend
of mine.

It seemed important for her that we met Richardt. Fritz and Hans felt my unease, but Hans nodded reassuringly.

C'mon, we can do this.

So we went downstairs. Frau Griezell had put her children to bed and a vinyl was playing on the turntable. Richardt had brought a bottle of *Schnapps.* As Frau Griezell poured the glasses, Richardt, Fritz and Hans talked as if they were old friends. As if they'd known each other for ever. This amazed me time and time again. Friendly as Richardt seemed, I was anxious to be found out and let the others do the talking. Consequently, I came across as shy. I got more self assured though as time went by.

Getting to know Frau Griezell's schedule was on the top of my list. She owned a bicycle with two children seats. The boy sat behind her and the girl in front. Generally, they left before 8am. On her way to work, she'd first drop off her children at school. After work, she'd pick them up and they got home around half past five. During the day time we had the house to ourselves.

If she was home, Frau Griezell could hear and see us leave and return from her ground floor apartment. To give Frau Griezell the impression that Fritz and my brother went to work every day, they both left the house before Frau Griezell. My schedule, I told her, was pretty much dependent on how I decided to plan my day. She knew better than to ask.

A couple of hours after Frau Griezell left for work, Fritz and Hans would come home. In the afternoon, in time before Frau Griezell and her children returned, they would leave again. Around 8pm, pretending to be exhausted from a long day's work, they returned home.

I was often on the road. I became pretty good at reading telltale signs indicating whom to trust and whom not to trust. At times looks could be deceiving. Neighbors in our street who knew Frau Griezell were convinced that we were *nazis*.

A home with a balcony flying a third Reich swastika flag could be hiding Jews or fighters in the resistance.

Someone I trusted usually knew someone they trusted who knew individuals who needed help; families and extended families needed to obtain ID cards, food vouchers, clothing, etc.

Frau Griezell felt relatively safe. Her *Reich* tenants, she felt, would be able to safeguard her. In her mind, our work made us important. Our connections even more so. Few people would dare mess with her. Living in the lion's den was a delicate balancing act, filled with risk. Every word I exchanged with Frau Griezell was weighed and deliberated over before spoken.

The nazi-regime considered the Dutch racially Aryan brothers. Hitler had chosen this option on ideological grounds; he considered the Dutch people of kindred spirit, part of the Aryan Herrenvolk or master race. That's why in Holland, the nazis at first installed a civilian administration instead of the usual military government as it had in the other occupied countries they had invaded. The nazis mistakenly anticipated a smooth integration of Holland into greater Germany or the Third Reich.

Fritz's parents were still hiding on the farm with that chatty woman. I went back to the kiosk and studied the rental listings again. When Fritz and I checked out the second floor of an old former canal side warehouse, the layout appealed to us. We decided that the landlord didn't need to know that his new tenants were Jewish. So, we rented the floor and brought Fritz's parents and aunt back from the countryside and moved them in. While at the farm, his mother's hair had turned white and she did not look Jewish any more. Even though she could get away with doing her own shopping, she mostly stayed indoors.

Fritz, Hans and Leo invested in bottles of French perfume. They bought as many bottles as they could find. Their intuition had been right. Every time our food supply ran low, they sold a bottle of perfume or bartered for food. This was a great help throughout the war. My in-laws also gave us goods to exchange for food.

Before the war, Fritz's father owned a fabric business. When fabrics were no longer available, the price skyrocketed on the black market. Just before the family was ordered to move up to Amsterdam, Fritz's father had the foresight to give the bolts of fabric to a friend for safekeeping.

As food became scarce, farmers became the go-to folks. Farmers bartered food for products that they in turn resold and made healthy profits from; like fabrics.

The Jews were ordered to list their valuables, including their bank accounts and balances. The Germans misappropriated the spoils and the Jews had no access to money. To keep them quiet, the Germans paid them a small amount until they were deported. The return train tickets for the guards and the one-way tickets (in the cattle cars) to the camps were paid with the monies stolen from the Jewish bank accounts.

Fritz's father needed money and wanted to sell some of the fabric bolts his friend stored for safekeeping. At the time Fritz was on a job and I decided to pick up the material. I never wrote down directions, names, phone numbers or any kind of information that could implicate others. So before traveling south to pick up a couple of fabric bolts, I memorized the friend's name, his address and directions.

I traveled at morning peak time. I made it a habit to pick an aisle seat. We left on time. After an hour or so, the train unexpectedly slowed down and finally came to a full stop. We were in between stations. A man sitting next to me at the window said to no one in particular that a pair of policemen were boarding the train at opposite ends. We knew that they'd slowly work their way towards the middle, checking documents. It could be a routine check, or they could be looking for someone. Passengers were told to open their suitcases.

I had no luggage, still I was anxious. When they got to me, I was asked where I was going. While handing over my ID, I answered that I worked for the *Wehrmacht* and that this was a work trip. The man next to me at the window flinched. The policeman was Dutch and as soon as he heard my German accent, he touched his cap and wished me a good day.

What will happen on the way back, when I have the bolts of material with me?

My heart rate picked up. Only after the security police got off at the next station and the train had picked up speed again, did I relax somewhat. The man next to me had gotten off and the passenger sitting across from me smiled at me. I smiled back, thinking he could be a collaborator, but he could also be on a mission to fight the occupation. You just didn't know. Appearances were so deceiving.

My hunch proved right. I couldn't just board the train with bolts of cloth under my arm. They were bound to be confiscated or worse. Fritz and my brother would have warned me, but they weren't around for a couple of days and I had taken it upon myself to do this.

I arrived at the station mid-day. I had about three hours to pick up the material and catch the train back to Amsterdam. After about a forty minute walk I rang the door bell. The friend had been expecting me. After a quick cup of tea, he handed me two bolts and showed me into a separate room. I took off my clothes and wrapped the two bolts of cloth around my body, securing the ends with safety pins. I put my clothes back on and my baggy coat over it all. I could hardly move. Wide coats were in fashion, so I looked overweight, if not pregnant.

During the train ride home, air-raid sirens sounded as allied bomber planes on their way to Germany breached the airspace above us. The train stopped and a man in a railroad uniform told us to quickly disembark and follow him away from the tracks. Fortunately, we continued the journey to Amsterdam a short while later. With the tightly wrapped bolts around my body I could barely move or breathe and being seated was very uncomfortable. Back in Amsterdam, Fritz had returned and I showed him what I had brought back. He was impressed.

***

Barbara

Hans's girlfriend Barbara (19) was two years younger than Hans. She was also born in Germany. In 1933, the year that Hitler became chancellor, Barbara's parents left Berlin for Amsterdam, where they joined Barbara's grandparents. When Barbara went to primary school in Amsterdam, she and

Margo Frank, sister of German refugee Anne Frank, were pupils in the same grade. The Frank family and Barbara's family lived close to each other. The parents and the daughters became friends.

Barbara took ballet classes before the war broke out. She was very talented and wanted to continue dancing as a career. There were more Jewish ballet students at the ballet school. After the nazis took control of Holland, the Jewish students stopped going to class. Mid 1944, all Jewish students had disappeared.

Hans explained to Barbara that those who disappeared were deported to concentration camps and murdered upon arrival. Barbara didn't believe him. It took a lot of explaining on Hans's part to convince her. After a while, Barbara understood that Hans kept himself well informed. He warned her that if she is caught, she will be deported. He suggested that he could try and arrange a new ID for her. She could then pass for a non-Jew, which in her case was not far fetched; she was German, Aryan looking with blonde hair and blue-eyes. But Barbara worried. What if she is caught? What will happen to her parents?

Either way, they will be sent to Poland and they will end up dead. Let me save you at least.

She thought about it and started asking questions.

Where will I live? How will I survive? What about food and money?

The fate of the men, women and children who had been deported, was a topic of debate. Murder or ethnic cleansing as it is called today, on an industrial scale that large, was a new concept, because it had never happened before. It was a first. So many people, including Jews believed that these were propaganda rumors.

Hans warned her that the police went from neighborhood to neighborhood picking up Jewish families for deportation and her street would be next. He sent a friend to go and get her, but her father kicked him down the stairs. He wouldn't hear of parting with his daughter. When the friend reported to Hans what had happened, he decided to go that night and get Barbara out of there himself.

Barbara's mother liked and trusted Hans enough to let her daughter leave with him. With her blessing, Hans hid Barbara in our father's factory, until I found her a boarding house outside of the city, where the manager 'forgot' to check her fake ID. I provided her with food stamps.

But as often happens when children and young adults are separated from their parents, Barbara misses her family terribly. She decided to take a huge risk and traveled back to the city to visit her family. Due to the evening curfew, she needed to stay over.

That night they heard banging on front doors two down from theirs. Four families were taken away. Parents and children disappeared never to be seen again. The peaceful evening was restored.

A neighbor came by and warned them that they were next. Hans had heard that too and decided to pick her up in the middle of the night. Thanks to her mother, Hans got Barbara out of there. All she brought with her was a piece of soap, a towel and a toothbrush.

At daybreak, German and Dutch police units drove into the neighborhood announcing over loudspeakers that all Jews still present had to gather outside. Earlier they had received a one-page list with items they were allowed to bring. Pets had to be left behind. That broke a lot of hearts. Barbara survived the war. Both her parents and her sister were deported and murdered.

Food had become scarce and rations were down to about 450 calories a day. The situation had changed from difficult to desperate.

***

Elsa

Needing to barter the cloth fabric for food, I planned a serious bike ride to the countryside, where farmers located south of the river still had some food to barter.

It was late summer and the weather would still allow for it. My bike needed a tune-up. Fritz oiled the chain, added air to the tires, made sure the lights were in working order, just in case I couldn't make the curfew and he fitted a pair of baskets on both sides of the rear wheel. There was a basket in the front as well. In short, he made sure that the ride wouldn't be too unpleasant.

That evening, Fritz insisted that I traveled with someone else. It was safer that way. He had asked an acquaintance to accompany me. Elsa was not Jewish. She was going to meet me in the early morning hours at a prearranged location. I didn't like the idea much and told him so. I was better off doing this sort of thing on my own, so I could keep my own tempo and didn't have to worry about another person. My brother agreed with Fritz, so I left it at that. It turned out to be a big mistake.

It was a summer's day. The war was in its third year. Although the Dutch weather could turn without a moment's notice, that day it was pleasantly cooperating. A few high clouds in an otherwise blue sky seemed not to want to be bothered with us. I reckoned that to get the job done leaving around 7am could get us back to the city before the 8pm curfew.

Unfortunately, the trouble started before we even left the city limit. My bike felt like new. Even with the bolts of material, I felt light like a feather. I noticed the tires or lack thereof on Elsa's bike. They were worn out. She was basically riding on rims. Sliding from side to side, she was having a terrible time remaining in control. We barely made any progress and so I suggested we switch bikes every half hour.

That worked well for a while, until it was my turn to switch back to my own bike and she refused. We had left the city behind us but still had long ways to go. I couldn't get into it with her. Starting a fight and drawing attention to ourselves was out of the question. I wasn't the fighting type anyway and so I let it be. I reminded myself that the most important thing was to return home safely.

Riding on rims was exhausting. It was wobbly and hard to keep steady. We barely spoke and it took about five hours instead of three to get to the location where I wanted to try and catch a row boat cross the river. My plan to make it back to Amsterdam before curfew faded fast.

Crossing the river was forbidden. But there were characters with rowing boats who were prepared to row across clandestinely for a fee, of course. Taking a chance was financially worth their while. They usually waited till the boat filled up. In a wooded area, at the end of a short sandy path that lead to the river, I saw the small rowing boat. The owner was smoking a self-rolled cigarette. It could accommodate five individuals and three bikes. Luckily we were the last two. As soon as the owner of the boat pocketed our passage and bike money, he pushed off. We were two women, a male and a boy, I reckon in his teens. Nobody said a word. It was eerily quiet, except for the sounds of birds singing and the oars gently splashing in and out of the water, momentarily disappearing below the surface. I was too nervous to enjoy the beauty of the natural surroundings. The adrenaline rush was unrelenting. Plenty of rumors around that some of the men who ferried people across betrayed them to the authorities waiting on the other side. Could this boat owner be trusted? He could make a nice little extra by reporting us.

Twenty minutes later we reached the other side. The owner offloaded our bikes and not wasting a moment, wished us good luck and immediately headed back. Out of breath from pushing our bikes up the steep side of the dike, we reached the top. Shocked we looked down the barrel of a *Mauser* rifle that a soldier in *Wehrmacht* uniform pointed at us.

Halt! he yelled in German, asking what we were doing there. I estimated him to be my age, nineteen or twenty. He seemed nervous and didn't wait for an answer.

Come with me.

He motioned with his rifle for us to start walking.

If you try anything, I will shoot.

I recognized his accent, it was the same as mine. I sounded cheeky when I asked him in German if he was from Cologne too. I forced myself to smile and joked with a heavy Cologne dialect that a guy from Cologne would never shoot a girl from Cologne. He relaxed somewhat and lowered his rifle.

Look, can't you let us go? We're hungry and here to barter with the farmers for food. Check the baskets. Just let us go.

He said he couldn't do that. Orders are orders. He told us to keep walking.

Where are you taking us?

To my command post. So, where in Cologne?

I mentioned the name of a street in a non-Jewish neighborhood, where a girlfriend of mine lived.

What are you doing here?

My dad got transferred to Amsterdam.

The teenager who was in front, held back until he walked next to me. He whispered to me that he was Jewish and on his way to a hiding place.

What do I do? he asked.

I told him to remain calm, to keep his mouth shut and not say a word. Not to anyone. I don't know why he trusted me.

The command post was billeted in the town hall. Just before entering the building, I asked the soldier to grant the teenager permission to remain with our bikes or they'll be stolen. That was fine. I expected the young lad to take off, as soon as we were inside, but he didn't understand.

The commander wanted to see our ID's. He asked us a bunch of questions and made notes. I told him the same looking-for-food story. Elsa and the man didn't speak German, so I translated. It was all very thorough, very German.

We were told to sit in the waiting area.

Thirty minutes later we were free to go. The soldier returned our ID's to us. The gentleman walked out and took off on foot, because his bike was confiscated on the spot.

For Elsa, it all had become too much; she could no longer contain her emotions and became hysterical.

I am scared. I don't want to get into trouble. I'm going to tell them that you're Jewish, Elsa said.

I kept calm. I knew that she was newly married and that she called her husband by his pet-name *little sheep*. I promised her that if she does something stupid, not only will it end badly for me, but she'll be arrested for keeping company with a Jew. If she screamed or drew attention in any way, she'll never see her *sheep* again.

Suddenly the soldier called me by my name. I told Elsa to go outside.

He told me to wait right there and disappeared momentarily. When he returned he had his hands full. He handed me a chunk of meat wrapped in paper and a typical German rye bread, also in paper. He also gave me a small bag of potatoes and two bottles of milk. I was speechless. He walked me to my bike. He noticed the flat tires and apologized that he couldn't help.

I divided his gifts over the baskets. I thanked him and said I thought that it was very nice of him. He whispered not to tell anyone, using a Cologne expression that meant something like don't even tell your dog.

He was my age. Before the war, we might have been friends. Suddenly I was surprised to hear myself asking him if later today he could maybe help us get back across the river to the other side. He said to meet him at 20:00 hours on the river bank. Dusk will have started. He told me his name was Claus and walked back into the building.

I now noticed the teenager who, instead of making himself scarce, still stood there, near the bicycles. I told him in Dutch to leave. He did.

Elsa got onto my bike and complained that it was heavier than before. The rest of the afternoon she kept quiet. Even so, it was a terrible experience. I worried all afternoon that she was going to betray me.

At the first farm, the farmer wanted nothing to do with us and told me so. One hour and two farms later, I was in luck. They wanted the materials that I had picked up a few days earlier for Fritz's father. It got me fifteen pounds of wheat grain.

While we were waiting at the riverbank for Claus to show up I told her that we needed to spend the night somewhere. She was scared and wanted to keep going after curfew. I had to convince her that we'd end up somewhere in a police cell. Elsa knew I was right.

What if that soldier doesn't show?

The sun had set and dusk took its time. Claus showed up as typically behooves the German *Pünktlichkeit*. His unit had a small river patrol craft. It lay moored hidden below some overhanging tree branches. I couldn't believe our luck. We boarded and he even helped us with our bikes. He moved to the wheel and started the engine. He showed off a little for me, I could tell. He smiled and gestured me to stand next to him. Halfway across to the other side we heard the now so familiar sound of monotone airplanes rumbling coming our way. They came from the east. Moments later some fifteen four-engine flying fortresses flew in formation heading west. I knew the Americans flew bombers in the day time and the Brits bombed Germany at night.

As we arrived at the north bank, he sounded sincere when he said he was sorry about not having the time to fix the tires. He moved the bikes off the boat and gentlemanly held out his hand as we disembarked. I thanked him again and he wished us good luck. Suddenly he asked what school I had attended in Cologne. It seemed more of an after-thought. I don't think he meant to trick me, but I was taken aback. I couldn't tell him the name of my Jewish school. I recalled the memories of those mean boys chasing me while calling me rotten Jew. Their school was located near *Neumarkt* or New Market. I pronounced it like the locals in a Cologne dialect and said "that *school in the Humboldtstrasse* near *Nümaat*. He smiled. *Humboldt Gymnasium.* Some of his friends had gone there. He tipped hit cap, turned the boat and headed back. We went our ways.

I was too drained to quibble with Elsa, so she rode my bike. She seemed still under duress and kept quiet, which suited me just fine. With her baskets now also filled, it was difficult for me to control her bike. All my energy went to pushing the pedals. It was absolutely overwhelming.

Fairly soon we passed a 'room for rent meals included sign' in the window of a private home. It was just after eight o'clock and I decided that I'd had enough excitement for one day.

Curfew ended by 6:00 am. I wanted an early start and told Elsa that we needed to get going at daybreak. She didn't react. We shared one room and I slept with one eye open and one ear alert. After breakfast, we climbed back onto our overloaded bicycles and started the long and perilous ride home around 7am.

It was late afternoon when I got home. Totally exhausted, but I knew I did good. The wheat grain to bake bread lasted for months. I gave the cash received for the bolts of material to Fritz. When I told him and Hans how I got the meat and the bottles of milk, they joked that Elsa had brought me luck after all.

As it turned out, we were six living together at this time; my fiancé Fritz and I, my brother Hans, his girlfriend and a third couple that was temporarily in hiding on our floor. I made the same trip a few months later. On my own this time and I managed to get back home that same evening.

***

The Walls have Ears

By 1944, there were no Jews left and the familiar round ups had come to a standstill. The few Jews who remained were in hiding or like us were in possession of forged papers. Those in charge of the deportations suspected that a few Jews had slipped through the net and tightened the screws.

Frau Griezell's intense hatred towards Jews saved our lives more than once.

One night two men rang the front door bell. Frau Griezell was getting ready for bed and had no intention of answering the door. But, when the bell rang a second time, she thought it was her soldier lover. So she put on her house coat and answered the door. Two men in civvies wanted to question her about her tenants. They were investigating information that she was hiding Jews. They were Dutch, but spoke in German. This gave her the advantage. Frau Griezell laughed. Obviously their information was absurd. She knew for a fact that her tenants were *Reich* Germans who worked for the *Gestapo*. What nonsense. She would never help Jews. She'd rather kill herself than help a Jew. Their accusation hit a nerve. She was disgusted. How could they suspect her of betraying the trust of the *Führer*. She convinced them and they wished her goodnight. She closed the door and heard them drive away. She never once doubted her own words.

In the morning, before Fritz and Hans left for 'work,' they knocked on her door. She told them what happened. Did she get the names on their badges? She didn't. Fritz told her that next time she must wake him up and he'll take care of it. How dare they trouble her at night. She appreciated it when he took charge that way. More than once did she confide in me that having us there gave her a feeling of security. We both benefited from this wildly volatile situation.

Two months later, the bell rang again. This time at 2 am. Two plain clothed men from the German Security Police were at the door. They addressed her in German. They had come to get the Jews who lived at this address. Offended, she told them that high ranking *Gestapo* officers rented the upstairs. She offered to wake them up, but there'll be hell to pay.

My tenants, she told them, are strongly connected to Berlin.

One of the men noticed an unopened piece of mail on a small accent table in the hallway. She handed it to him. He opened it and read it, then gave it to his mate to read, who next handed it back to Frau Griezell. They were satisfied.

In the afternoon, as she handed me our mail, she told me the story. My heart pounded so hard, my chest felt like it was about to burst open. I kept quiet for a moment. Then I told her that waking Fritz in the middle of the night would not have ended well for them. Inside of me I was trying to suppress a surge of absolute panic.

That evening, when Fritz and I were alone, I handed him the letter in the opened envelope and told him what happened. He smiled.

It's time to mail myself another letter.

Split pea soup

Frau Griezell had grown quite fond of Fritz. He was always ready to lend a hand. If she needed a favor or something around the house needed fixing, she'd call on him. Times were tough and she didn't want workmen's eyes wandering inside her home. It was not a good time for having strangers over.

One cold winter evening Frau Griezell was in the kitchen with her two children preparing their evening meal. Fritz, Hans and I were upstairs. The door from our living room to the stairwell was ajar. The smell of split pea soup filled the stairwell. The doorbell rang and as we tended to do, we stopped talking and listened. We heard her open the front door. We couldn't hear who was at the door but within moments we heard Frau Griezell's voice hysterically screaming out for Fritz to come downstairs. Startled, Hans and I stayed at the top of the steep narrow staircase, out of sight.

A Dutch detective had come to pick Frau Griezell up. She was accused of black-market trading, supposedly in coffee, alcohol and cigarettes. The detective ordered Frau Griezell to get her coat, because she was coming with him to the police station. Frau Griezell was terrified out of her mind. She yelled again for Fritz. He greeted the policeman politely in German, using a tone of respect, but at the same time making it clear who outranks whom.

What is the purpose of your visit?

But before the man could answer, Fritz turned to Frau Griezell.

It's freezing out. Why don't you offer this gentleman a bowl of your freshly made soup?

She nodded, trying to hide her desperation. Fritz invited the man in and he eagerly obliged. From the top of the stairs I heard what was going on. I was amazed at Fritz's daring. Fritz took the man's coat and suggested that Frau Griezell hang it in the living room, over a chair near the fireplace. She did. In the kitchen Frau Griezell served both of them a bowl of delicious soup and a slice of home made bread, thanks to the wheat grain we at times provided her with. She closed the kitchen door with some excuse that the children were asleep and came halfway up the staircase. She whispered my name. When she saw me at the top of the stairs she pleaded with me to please give her a hand. I followed her down into the living room where she opened the door of a cabinet. It was bursting with unopened cartons of cigarettes and bottles of booze. I was truly surprised, but didn't comment. She wanted me to help move everything upstairs to our floor. While Fritz and the investigator were in the kitchen, I hurried up and down the staircase, handing Hans the contraband at the top of the stairs. We heard the door to the kitchen open. In the hallway Fritz shook the man's hand.

***

A Dangerous Balancing Act

In 1944, the Americans land in Italy. The Third Reich victory is no longer an obvious fact. The winter of 1944 was brutally cold. The shelves in the stores were empty. The nazi-occupier sent all foodstuffs to the German soldiers on the front. The Dutch people were so desperate, they raided the bulb fields, dug the bulbs up, boiled and ate them. Disregarding the curfew, people hunted for wood and fuel. They stole the wooden blocks between train and tram rails. They broke into vacant homes and axed wooden bannisters using them to feed fires for cooking in self-made stoves. They searched for driftwood along the riverbanks, dried it and used it to feed their fireplaces. Farmers traded table silver and linen for vegetables and flour, until they too ran out.

One rainy afternoon, a few young men active in the resistance were visiting Hans and Fritz. They were sitting around the table playing cards. That day, Frau Griezell returned home earlier than usual. We didn't know she came home until we heard knocking on our door to the hallway. We froze. Fritz got up and opened the door.

What is going on here? Don't you have to go to work today?

Standing in the doorway, Frau Griezell asked Fritz.

Without a blink he had his answer ready.

Frau Griezell, we have visitors over from Berlin. So we took the day off. Would you like to come in? Please sit down. Let me pour you a drink. He stood up and offered her his chair. He introduced her to the new faces around the table. This conversation was spoken entirely in German and felt completely natural.

You, me, these guys, we all work for our *Führer*. She looked at the new faces and couldn't help but noticing that they were definitely no Aryan looking types.

Very Jewish looking, she joked.

They laughed with her. My cousin proved to be gifted like Fritz. He took his wallet out and showed her a photo. I may be dark, but look at my brother. He showed her a photo of an Aryan looking man, blonde and blue eyed in a cavalry dress uniform standing in front of his horse.

That's my brother, fighting for our *Führer*. I haven't heard from him in a while, he added in a sad tone of voice.

Frau Griezell felt for him and commented that surely he was going to be fine.

The *Führer* will keep him safe.

We raised our glasses and toasted to the *Führer*. Frau Griezell added her own version to the toast.

And to the downfall of all Jews.

We raised our glasses again and toasted with her.

Her children weren't home and there was no reason for Frau Griezell to rush downstairs. Fritz offered her another drink. She liked socializing with us; the young men were upbeat, cracking an occasional joke at the expense of the Allies and the Jews. On the wall she noticed a large political wall map of Europe, covered with swastika flag pins. She got up and stood in front of it, studying it, trying to make sense of it.

Mr. Sander, the owner of the cigar shop across the street was an avid anti-nazi. He didn't hide it either. In his eyes, we were nazi *Krauts*. He never wanted to sell us anything. He was rigid and rude to us in a sly kind of way. Whenever I entered his shop, he looked the other way.

My brother came home with a large political wall map he bought at Mr. Sander's cigar shop; *A Wall Map of Germany, 1944*.

Frau Griezell stood looking at that wall map attentively. Hans had pinned swastika flags on locations, indicating where Hitler's troops were fighting major battles. Fritz stood up and joined her. As he stood next to her, they both looked at the map. Fritz waited a moment before asking her if she understood what it is that she was looking at. She asked him to explain. He explained the geopolitical state of Europe in general and the major battles in particular. He knew the names of the generals and talked about the enormity of the logistics of winning a war. He explained the operational and tactical decisions always to the benefit of the *Führer*.

He turned to the guys at the table and announced with a straight face that Hitler was the best military strategists bar none that Europe has ever known. His name would never be forgotten. He called for another toast to the *Führer*. The facts were quite different.

There had been another attack on Hitler's life. And again it had failed. But even so, the tide had turned. Even after the Allies had landed in France and the Soviets were making headway in Poland, Hitler refused to accept his losses. The German army was retreating on all fronts.

Frau Griezell interrupted him.

Fritz, I love it when you talk about our *Führer*. At least you talk about the good things he does. Hans is so pessimistic. He always warns me that we should not be so optimistic, because the *Führer* can make mistakes too. But then when I talk to you, you always tell me not to worry. Do you really believe that our *Führer* will win the war for us?

Of course. Just look what he has achieved in Poland.

Fritz comforted her and with his hand he outlined Poland on the map. That's all ours now.

This was of course incorrect. Fritz concealed the fact that the Soviet Union had become an ally **after the Germans attacked the Soviet Union in 1941 and that** now the Soviet troops had almost reached the Polish city of Warsaw. Fritz didn't mention that, instead he assured Frau Griezell that she and her children had nothing to worry about.

Our *Führer* has never been in better shape.

He added she should not listen to anyone claiming otherwise. And of course, nobody dared to claim otherwise. That would be considered treason. Frau Griezell was over the moon. She had to go and pick up her children. She wished us all a good evening and our visitors from Berlin a good stay in Amsterdam and went downstairs.

We never for a minute let our guard down. Trepidation was a constant companion behind our smiles. Vigilance had become second nature. If Frau Griezell got arrested for harboring Jews, she would of course claim that she didn't know. But who would believe her? So that was the state of affairs; any moment in freedom, was a good moment.

Frau Griezell shared her plans with me over a cup of coffee one Sunday morning. She was thinking of moving. She wanted to start a boarding house somewhere nearby and because we had been great tenants, she wanted to know if we were interested in moving with her. In those days when hearing news, I always tried to figure out how that would impact us. Was that good or bad news. What did it mean for us personally? I started by thanking her for the compliment and returned it. I assured her that we would miss her, but I would visit her for sure. I then shared with her that Fritz and I were planning on getting married. Would it be at all possible to have the ground-floor lease put in our name?

And so it happened. We ended up renting both floors.

Hans had befriended a German soldier, a deserter from the army. He was a carpenter by trade. The two got along and trusted each other. As soon as Frau Griezell and her children moved out, Hans hired him to build a hiding space below the first floor hallway. He made the space accessible through a hatch. Having a place to hide was a good feeling. We timed and clocked it at thirty seconds to get in there from the moment the front doorbell rang. Also in the hallway, below the staircase in the wall, he constructed a small space, the size of a small safe, where we hid all kinds of illegal and counterfeit paperwork; stolen passports, ration cards, swastika stamps and stolen stationary.

The food I managed to get my hands on was mainly for the folks hiding in our house and for my mother and Fritz's parents. I tried my best to find edibles for those I had found a hiding place for. My bike rides to the countryside decreased. Even the farmers ran out of food.

***

Final Reckoning

The anti-nazi newsletter 'Het Parool' (The Password or The Motto) originated as an illegal eight-page news bulletin. If you were caught with a copy, you were done for. In 1944, fifteen story contributors were betrayed and sentenced to time in concentration camps. About every two weeks, 100,000 copies were distributed by members of the Dutch resistance.

Every couple of weeks I helped distribute illegal copies of a stenciled newsletter. At different locations, I would pick up a stack of newsletters and slip them into my shoulder bag.

I didn't use my bike, that would make delivering them too conspicuous. At the junction of the

Olympiaplein and *Stadionweg*, I noticed two German soldiers on the sidewalk across the street, walking my direction. They noticed me too. I could tell, because one gestured slightly with his chin towards me and the other one now looked my way too. I was pretty certain that they were talking about me. I had light curly blond hair and I was quite attractive.

I crossed the street and approached them to ask for directions.

Don't panic. They can smell fear.

I asked in German, of course with a friendly smile.

Do you know the Utrechtsedwarsstraat? I asked.

How do I get there from here? I'm lost.

They were friendly enough and went out of their way to tell me.

I walked for hours through Amsterdam, pushing copies of the latest newsletter through mail slots. Reading that the Allies were making headway gave the Dutch hope. I often had dreams about my bags being searched and being interrogated about the copies of the newsletter that were discovered.

It was about five in the afternoon and I was on my way to catch a tram to visit my mother. I couldn't visit her as often as I liked to for fear of compromising her situation and that of the host family. But between my brother, Fritz and me, we checked up on her every so often and made sure that she was okay. This time I was carrying a ration card in my purse for her host family. The card was made out in their name. Getting caught with a ration card showing a name other than your own, was a serious crime.

I hurried across the city center square, today the famous *Leidseplein*, and headed towards the tram stop. Suddenly I noticed the sound of footsteps on the cobblestones trailing behind me. As I increased my tempo, so did the footsteps. I was sure I wasn't imagining it, but to avoid any type of confrontation, I didn't want to turn around. Then suddenly I felt two taps on my shoulder. This is it. I'm done for. I turned around. The man I stood face to face with belonged to the dreaded *Grüne Polizei* police force. I was eighteen years old, Jewish and terrified. And, intensely aware that I couldn't show it.

'Grüne' means green in German. The Grüne Polizei was the dreaded German police force. Their nick name referred to their green uniforms. They assisted their Dutch counterpart with operations involving tracking down Jews.

I looked into the eyes of what to me seemed an older man, perhaps in his mid-fifties.

So miss, where are you headed? I lied and told him that I was on my way home.

Can I walk with you?

Somewhat relieved, I thought he just wants to flirt a bit. He didn't wait for an answer. What if someone sees me with this creep in his green uniform? Turning the corner, across from the much beloved *Vondelpark*, he stopped in front of a row of typical Amsterdam canal homes where the canal itself had been filled in around the late 1890's, and was now a road adorned on both sides by reverent mature chestnut trees. He stopped and pointed at one of the homes, telling me that's where he lives with a few other gentlemen.

Come on in. I'll make you a cup of coffee.

It sounded more like an order than an invitation. I wasn't sure what to do. If I refused, he would ask for my papers.

Don't panic. They can smell fear.

I'll come in for a moment, but I do need to get home. It's getting late.

I'll get you home. Don't you worry miss.

Think, I told myself, think!

I wasn't sure how to get out of it this time. What could I do?

I'll come in for a moment, but I really need to get home. It is almost eight o'clock. If you like, I can stop by tomorrow for a cup of coffee.

I followed him in and acted relaxed while my heart was racing and my blood was pumping full force though every inch of my body. As soon as he closed the front door, he started getting touchy-feely. It was very frightening. I told him I'd be back the following day for sure, then we would have more time. He seemed fixated.

But you must really come. Promise me that you'll come.

He raised his voice.

You can't not come. That's not how we do things around here.

104

I know that, I said. Acting offended I assured him that my promise was a promise.

I must be able to rely on you.

Feigning interest for a row of photos on the wall, I slowly moved towards the front door. When I was close enough, I opened it and stepped into the street.

See you tomorrow, I told him as I hurried away. But he didn't give up and followed me.

Let me walk you home.

Now I was panic-stricken, because I couldn't go home. As if on cue, I saw an approaching tram and took my chance.

Ah, there is my tram. See you tomorrow, bye! He grabbed my coat, turned me around and kissed me hard on my lips. He was of course much stronger and I couldn't just push him off of me.

Please, let go of me, I pleaded quietly.

I'll see you tomorrow, I yelled louder,

Overtaken by my resolve, he let go of me. I jumped aboard the tram just before the doors closed. To this day, I believe that some serious lucky stars got me out of this quandary.

I lived in a continuous state of apprehension over getting caught and was under no illusion that it couldn't happen to me. We learned to live with that looming doom. Upending the occupation and saving lives kept me busy throughout the war.

There was always someone who knew someone who knew someone somewhere, who needed help.

My cousin, the one who showed Frau Griezell the photo of his Aryan brother on a horse, asked me if I could find his brother-in-law a safer housing situation.

One time I was asked to pick up a couple and take them to a different location. When I went to pick them up, I rang the front door bell. I followed the man who opened the door into a room where parents and their children were gathered. No one in the room spoke. One of the men in the room I recognized was my mother's cousin, the lawyer from the Jewish Council, who had told my mother to just pack a suitcase for her and for my brother and me and report for deportation to the East, meaning Germany or Poland. He basically had advised my mother not to go into hiding, and here he was with his wife and child, hiding. When I entered the room, both he and his wife showed no sign of recognition. I appreciated that. Instead, he got up and left the room. Within a few minutes I left with the husband wife pair following me at a distance, walking to their new hiding place. Someone not Jewish brought them their suitcase a few days later.

And so the war dragged on. I or anyone I knew, never expected to wake up one day to a horrid system as foreign and inhuman as the one we were caught up in against our will. To me and those around me, it was evident that we needed to keep fighting. So, I continued following my intuition and helped where help was needed. The circle of people who needed help kept growing.

My father had been relatively safe for some time, thanks to paperwork he managed to get from Bukovina, his father's country of origin. But towards the end of 1944, he too received a letter in which he was ordered to report for work in Germany. He asked if I could find a hiding place for him. While in hiding, he had no income and I had to find another way to help my mother.

Report a Jew! Reward: 7.50 guilders per person.

Hans and Fritz needed blank passports. I never asked them what for. Just as they didn't ask me for details when I needed something. I met with my contact who throughout the war had supplied me with food vouchers. It took a couple of weeks before he got back to me and told me where to pick them up.

***

Collaborators

Sometimes Fritz accompanied the individuals who wanted to leave the country to the Belgian border, other times Hans or Leo traveled with them. They moved on trains in threes or fours and didn't interact. On one of those journeys, Leo got arrested.

As Hans and Fritz were getting ready to leave for a border journey, a nazi-collaborator asked for help to cross the border. We had been warned about this guy and were expecting him. We fed him incorrect information and moved the actual date of departure up. Together with half a dozen plainclothes police units, he waited at the train station for hours.

All together, we helped close to a hundred people cross the border. On the other side of the border in Belgium, local contacts would help them on their way to their next destination, Switzerland or France.

There were moments we shared a joke and had a proper laugh. But these moments were always accompanied by a sense of dread and apprehension. Always keeping our eyes and ears open, making sure we were not followed or overheard. Sometimes the threat came from within a resistance network. If a member of an illegal movement was betrayed and arrested, torture or deportation threats could cause them to drop a name.

My brother and his mates keenly followed the latest news. Someone somewhere listened to the illegal BBC news broadcasts. Fritz and my brother often came home with news on how the Allies were making progress.

***

1945

The winter months at the start of 1945 were brutal. Temperatures dipped far below zero. The east-west flowing Rhine river divides Holland into the North and the South. The South had been liberated by the Allies. The North had no food and no fuel. The nazis fought hard to hold on to the land north of the river. Their tactics included blocking transports from the liberated South. The blockade lasted for six weeks and caused the greatest famine in the history of the country. People hunted for wood to fuel their coal stoves which they used to stay warm. And in darkness, men removed tram and train sleeper woods. Wooden staircases and railings in abandoned homes were looted for wood; parents sent their children out to comb the riversides for driftwood. The hunger was present anywhere and everywhere twenty-four hours a day. Many people died as a result. At this time, I was busy trying to score coal and food items. Prices had soared. The black market was thriving.

***

Liberation Anxiety

Germans and Dutch collaborators got ready to leave for Germany. Generally, collaborators were divided into three categories; political, financial and personal. Mobs shamed personal collaborators publicly. Dutch women who had befriended the nazi-enemy intimately were considered traitors and held down while their heads were shaven, after which they were paraded through the streets and jeered at. They were smeared with tar, stripped down half-naked or marked with swastikas, using paint or lipstick. Between 1940 and 1945, about

140.000 Dutch 'Kraut girls' yielded some 13,000 babies.

We had played a very dangerous game to stay alive. With the liberation of the entire country approaching, we felt another kind of pressure mounting.

Our neighbors knew no better than that we were German nazis or *Krauts* (short for *sauerkraut* or sour cabbage). We needed witnesses who knew about our situation and could protect us from an angry and misguided mob after the liberation.

A few months before the liberation, I received a tip that the police were about to raid the cigar shop across the street. The fiercely anti-Fascist and short tempered owner Mr. Sanders, had been betrayed. The *Gestapo* had been informed that he was keeping uniforms for the Domestic Armed Forces in his basement.

The Domestic Armed Forces were several resistance groups that were deployed to maintain law and order after the country was liberated.

I crossed the street and entered the cigar shop. Mr. Sanders stood behind the counter, helping a customer. As usual he ignored me. When the customer left, I whispered that I needed to speak to him privately. Other customers came and went and he repeated several times in a curtly fashion that I could see that he was busy. I told him that it was important. He replied that I should come back

110

another day. So I waited until I was alone with him. Quietly he motioned with his head for me to follow him. He turned around, moved aside a curtain that hid a room behind the counter. I followed him.

Mr. Sanders, I am here to tell you that we are German Jews and active in the resistance. Frau Griezell, our landlady, had no idea about us. His jaw dropped. After his initial shock, I told him why I had come.

I came to warn you. Through our contacts, I know you are keeping a supply of Domestic Armed Forces uniforms and a stack of guns in your basement. Someone ratted you out. This place is going to get raided. All of it has to be removed by tonight.

He was speechless. I told him about the hiding space below the floor in our hallway. He agreed. That night we moved it all and just in time. Early morning, around 3 o'clock, we woke up from the noise of the police banging on his front door and the glass shattering of his shop window. With all the evidence gone, they left a couple of hours after searching the shop and his home above the shop.

We became friendly with Mr. Sanders and his wife. They started visiting us. She brought us a few home made cookies from the flour she had managed to save. Mr. Sanders understood that the situation we were in was pretty dangerous.

A few days before we anticipated the liberation, he moved in with us to keep the neighborhood mob at bay. He joked that he felt safer with us *Krauts* as he called us affectionately, than in his own home. He had refused to turn in his radio, even though the penalty could be execution. So, we listened to the news on the BBC and were able to remain informed about the progress the Allies were making.

September 1944, liberation by the Allies was expected at any moment. Nazi-collaborators fled to Germany. A railroad strike made fleeing and transporting of soldiers difficult. During the freezing cold winter of 1944, in Amsterdam alone, some 2,300 civilians died due to lack of food, fuel and medicines. The second week of May 1945, first the Brits, then the Canadians were welcomed as liberators. On Tuesday May 8 1945, the occupying nazi-regime officially capitulated. Japan continued fighting in the Pacific theater and only surrendered in September of 1945.

Many nations around the world were touched by World War II. The combatants were grouped into two main factions: Allied and Axis powers.

The main Allies included: The United States, Great Britain, the Soviet Union and China. Siding with the Allies were: Denmark, Norway, Holland, Belgium, France, Luxembourg, Canada, Australia, New Zealand, Poland, Czechoslovakia, Ethiopia, Greece, Yugoslavia, Philippines, India, South Africa, Brazil, Turkey, Morocco, Mongolia, and Mexico.

The main Axis powers included: Germany, with partners Italy and Japan. Siding with the Axis powers were Finland, Romania, Hungary, Slovakia, Yugoslavia, Iran and Bulgaria.

Every country had its own reasons why they chose one side over the other. Their choices depended on internal politics, agendas, relations with neighboring countries, etc. Several countries switched sides halfway.

After we were liberated, Frau Griezell was told by our neighbors who she had remained friends with, that we were Jews. It must have hit her like a bombshell. However, this news did not keep her from ringing our door bell one day towards the end of 1945. She came to tell us that she was going to emigrate. She was joining her husband in America. And she didn't want to leave without saying goodbye. It was a strange goodbye, now that the tables were turned.

***

Liberated

The massive crowds in the streets showed overwhelming joy. Infantry soldiers handed out cookies, chocolate bars and cigarettes. Women jumped onto tanks rolling into the cities and embraced the soldiers. Men, women and children sang and danced as musicians played live music in the streets.

Celebrations throughout the country lasted all summer. Almost everyone was mad with joy. But not everyone felt liberated. Lots of people had been killed. Many women were waiting for their prisoner-of-war husbands to return. Jews who survived their hiding ordeal, were eagerly waiting for family members, relatives and friends to return. They were seen waiting for hours on train stations' platforms. It is said that when the war was finally over, their pain and their hurt started all over again for those who were left wondering what had happened to their loved ones who were deported by train to the concentration camps.

Suffice to say that we too were overjoyed that the war had finally ended, but we did not dare go outside. We were terrified of revenge actions. The next couple of days proved to be days of reckoning. We stayed away from the windows. It took time before we felt it was safe to leave the house. Moving freely outside felt strange. The day that Mr. Sander moved back into his own home was the moment it felt that the war had truly come to an end.

By the summer of 1945, it became clear to the Jewish survivors that deported family members, relatives and friends would never return. They were gone. People didn't like to say 'murdered.' The few Jews who did survive the camps were received coldly by the government and the Dutch people. They were processing their own war experiences and showed little interest in the losses that the Jews had suffered.

My mother and Fritz's parents moved in with us shortly after we were liberated. Fritz and I were living together, still unmarried. This was not something they were happy about. On December 24, 1945, my father-in-law brought home a rabbi to marry us, right then and there. We quickly called upon a group of friends. Including a couple we helped hide and whose five sons survived the war; for each son I had found a separate hiding place and each son survived. It was with great joy that we met again. Survivors from the camps had cheated death, only to return and find that they had lost everything; their homes had been sold and the new owners had no intention of moving out. Often times the survivors returned to their last address and the new owners opened the door while wearing the clothes or jewelry the deported Jews had hidden in the house. Returning personal or valuable items was out of the question.

Fritz and I welcomed those who had nowhere to go, to come and stay with us. Our friend Leo who had been arrested on one of his many assignments, was released from prison and barely looked alive; he was emaciated. He too moved in with us for a while.

***

Picking up the Pieces

I wanted to remain in Holland and soon after liberation, I applied for Dutch citizenship. Being granted citizenship meant a lot. Half my life I had been stateless. Having found a country that would have me was a great relief. Citizenship makes you feel protected for all the obvious reasons. Our rights had been taken from us. Now that I was legal again, I felt that I could get on with my life.

When the end of the war was in sight, Fritz, Hans and I discussed our plans for after war. Hans had saved up a little money and went looking to buy a number of sewing machines. I liked the idea of designing, and Fritz and Hans liked the manufacturing and selling part of the business. Hans borrowed two sewing machines and my mother gave me hers. Right after the war there was no fabric available, but Fritz had a knack for finding enough to get started. Gradually the supply stabilized.

So Fritz took care of buying the fabrics, I designed and sewed and Hans handled the financial side of the business. I worked from home. The downstairs living room turned into an atelier. Within two years we had fifteen sewing machines. Business was good.

Fritz and I had two children, a daughter and a son. With the sewing shop at home, our living space became too small. I wanted to rent a workspace somewhere in the neighborhood and move the atelier there. I found a suitable studio not too far away. Our home became a real home for the first time.

In 1953, Fritz and I decided to go our separate ways. I withdrew from the business and started over. Keeping the children in mind, I wanted to be home when they got home from school and so I decided to work from home again. I started out designing and sewing blouses. That went very well. But, as it turned out it was not much of a challenge and after a while I was bored out of my mind. Then I gathered the courage and took the plunge.

**

Haute Couture

I was interested in High Fashion and Fritz Heijmans was the top designer within the Dutch fashion industry. I found his work absolutely exceptional. It took me a while to gather the courage and call him. Finally, in 1963 I chanced it.

I said, Mr. Heijmans, you don't know me, but I know your work. I think your work is amazing. I want to work for you. May I come and visit you sometime?

I was ecstatic and full of optimism when he invited me to his atelier.

Fritz Heijmans came across as a business man. Skipping the small talk, he found a piece of crumpled up paper and swiftly sketched the outlines of a dress.

Take the measurements of that mannequin over there and show me what you've got. Come back when it's halfway ready and I'll take a look.

He handed me the sketch, got up and momentarily disappeared and returned with a piece of material. I was beyond thrilled.

At home I studied his very basic sketch. It left a lot to the imagination. I made a cup of tea and went straight to work. When the dress was half way ready, I went back to his atelier. The dress fitted the mannequin flawlessly. Fritz hired me on the spot. Sometimes after work we would go for a drink. He would often grab a coaster and sketch on it. He handed me the sketch and the material, and I ran with it. This is how we worked together for many years and every single time I loved the challenge. Many years later, he told me that from the day I set foot in his studio, I had not annoyed him for a moment. Surprisingly so, he added. I worked long hours and loved it. Fritz turned out to be quite a generous man They were good times. Work was fulfilling, the children did well and once a week I played a game of tennis.

For years, I believed that I had successfully left the war behind me. But there's only so long anguish and distress can be ignored. Grief and agony finally caught up with me. For one, I never really felt liberated. The tensions and fears I had experienced during the war continued to rage in my head. I was able to suppress the exhaustion the war years had brought about, but at long last, the long working hours had started to drain me. I continued working, but reduced the hours. Until 1978, I participated in all Heymans fashion shows.

All in all, the dark years of the war were followed by a career that lasted twenty-three wonderful years. At the age of 97, I look back on my life with great gratitude for the love I received from family, friends and strangers.

In 1947, 98% of all the party registered nazis were back at work. Even high ranking SS officials were able to build a career after the war as doctors, judges, teachers, professors, civil servants or journalists.

***

The Aftermath

My parents divorced after the war. My father remarried in 1948. He co-managed a movie rental company and in 1951, he owned a skirt factory in Düsseldorf, Germany. A few years later he started a moderately successful seat-belt business. He passed away in Amsterdam in 1972. At 95 years old, my mother passed away peacefully, also in Amsterdam.

Long after the war was over, I dreamed that some bounty hunter collaborator had found my brother and intended to hand him over to the nazis. I dreamed of the hiding place in our hallway that my brother had made after Frau Griezell had moved out. In my dreams I was always crawling in there and couldn't get the cover to fully close. I think back to those fearful times we endured and how we always had to be quick on our toes. Never letting our guard down, always having an answer at the ready.

As an acknowledgment for my activities in the resistance, I received the Dutch Resistance Memorial Cross. I am quite proud of receiving that honor. In addition, I obtained my Dutch citizenship.

In 2008, Pieter Landweer's granddaughter appealed in an article to readers who had known her grandfather, to please contact her. Her mother had just passed away and she was left with questions about her grandfather. I wrote her a letter and invited her over for a cup of tea.

There were many different Resistance groups. Members came from various religious and political backgrounds. Each had their ways of fighting the enemy; with weapons, sabotage at work, in the office, etc. Pieter Landweer used his office as a battleground. When members of one of the many Resistance groups organized a break-in at a Citizens Registration Office, they stole a large number of identity cards. Pieter Landweer had been involved. He paid for it with his life. We were shocked to learn that the Sicherheitsdienst had arrested him. Six weeks before the liberation of the south of Holland, Pieter Landweer was executed.

Righteous Among the Nations is an honorific used by the State of Israel to describe non-Jews who, for altruistic reasons, risked their lives in order to save Jews from extermination by the nazis.

I successfully spearheaded the request for Pieter Landweer to receive the honorific *Righteous Among the Nations*. His granddaughter traveled to Israel to receive the award on his behalf.

It turns out that we weren't the only secret in the street where we rented from Frau Griezell. Some neighbors hid resistance fighters, others hid Jews.

It is truly remarkable that we were not betrayed. Especially since we now know that the largest number of Jews betrayed by friends, neighbors or acquaintances occurred in Holland. More so than in Berlin or any other nazi-occupied country.

I donated my bag used for smuggling illegal documents and newspapers to the Resistance Museum in Amsterdam. Today, when watching families on television risking their lives for wanting to enter the safety of another country, my own memories are rekindled. I feel so powerless and a sense of sadness for the coming generations. It gets harder and harder to fight the sinister forces determined to disrupt the process of democracy.

I hope that this story inspires the younger readers to fight against racism and anti-Semitism. I would like to share with you the following quote:

"Remember, democracy never lasts long. It soon wastes, exhausts, and murders itself. There never was a democracy yet that did not commit suicide."
- John Adams, 2nd president of the United States (1735-1826)

***

Lili in 1940

Lili in 1942

The coaster with scribble (l) and the dress (r) that started Lili's career in haute couture or high fashion.

For more Holocaust/WWII memoir stories in this series please visit:
Amazon.com
BN.com

***